FRIEDMAN ON GALBRAITH

FRIEDMAN ON GALBRAITH

and on Curing the British Disease

MILTON FRIEDMAN

Nobel Laureate 1976
Paul Snowden Russell
Distinguished Service
Professor of Economics,
University of Chicago.

THE FRASER INSTITUTE
1977

Canadian Cataloguing in Publication Data
Friedman, Milton, 1912-
Friedman on Galbraith

London ed. (Institute of Economic Affairs) has title: From Galbraith to economic freedom.
Bibliography: p.
ISBN 0-88975-015-7 pa.

1. Galbraith, John Kenneth, 1908-
2. Great Britain—Economic conditions—1945- I. Fraser Institute, Vancouver, B.C. II. Title.
HB119.G33F75 330.1 C77-002107-7

First published in the U.K. by the Institute of Economic Affairs, January 197
First published in Canada by the Fraser Institute, April 1977
Canadian edition reprinted July 1977

Printed in Canada

Contents

Preface to the Canadian Edition

This book contains two essays by this year's Nobel Laureate, Professor Milton Friedman. They were delivered as lectures in the U.K. during the latter part of 1976 and were recently published in the U.K. by the Institute of Economic Affairs, London. The subject matter of these essays is of critical interest to Canadians and the Fraser Institute is pleased to be able to make them available to Canadian readers.

Currently, the Canadian Broadcasting Corporation is broadcasting a television series about the evolution of economics. This series is hosted by Professor John Kenneth Galbraith and in order to assess Galbraith's treatment of this evolution properly it is essential that the viewer have both a grasp of Galbraith's view of economics and the economist's view of Galbraith. In the first essay in this volume Professor Friedman, who has just been accorded the highest honour that the scientific community confers on its members, provides a non-technical view of Galbraithian economics and Galbraith as an economist.

The second essay deals with the steps necessary if Britain (and any other country suffering from the British disease) is to recover from its current desperate circumstances. Although this essay is perhaps of less immediate relevance to Canadians, it clearly points out the necessity to adopt gradualist corrective policies now before the more jarring policies currently required in the U.K. are necessary here. In addition, the principles that Professor Friedman develops in the second essay and in response to questions are of immediate Canadian interest.

In his Preface to the U.K. edition, Mr. Arthur Seldon of the Institute of Economic Affairs, provided a concise survey of the essays and it is reproduced here for reader convenience.

The Fraser Institute is honoured to have the opportunity to publish Professor Friedman's thoughts on these matters. However, owing to the independence of the author, the views expressed by him may or may not conform severally or collectively with those of the members of the Institute.

Michael Walker

April, 1977

Preface

AS PART of its educational purpose in explaining the light that economists can shed on industrial and government policy the Institute is reprinting as *Occasional Papers* essays or addresses judged of interest to a wider audience than those to which they were originally addressed. Occasional Paper 49 comprises the substance of two talks delivered to IEA audiences by Professor Milton Friedman on 31 August and 1 September, 1976. They are published together because, although they may appear to be on widely different themes, they can be seen in natural sequence. The first was an appraisal of the thinking of Professor John Kenneth Galbraith; the second was a discussion of the steps that would be required to be taken in passing from the present condition of the British economy to a freer market system.

It is possible to see they form a sequence insofar as the teaching of Professor Galbraith would appear to lead away from the general structure of a market economy. His recurrent critique of the conduct of industry has consistently pointed to more government control of the economy.

His analysis and conclusions are now contested in this *Paper* by Professor Friedman who, on the contrary, argues for a gradual advance to a freer economy. The first talk can be seen as an examination of the case for moving towards a more regulated economy, and the second as an analysis of the steps in moving away from a regulated to a more market-oriented economy.

Professor Friedman's central critique of Professor Galbraith reflects the characteristic approach of the Chicago school of which he is the now world-acknowledged head.

He examines Professor Galbraith's main complaints against the industrial system in a series of books going back over 25 years, and rejects them on the ground that they are based on hypotheses that, when tested by appeal to the evidence, are shown to be unfounded. In support of his critique he refers to the writings of American and British economists: Professors George Stigler, Harold Demsetz and Robert Solow of America and Professors G. C.

Allen, John Jewkes and Sir Frank McFadzean of Britain. Since the writings of Professor Galbraith are far better publicised than the works of economists who think his work is flawed, we have added extracts from several of them (in 'panels' to distinguish them from Professor Friedman's text) so that readers can judge the two sides.

In addition to the economist critics of Professor Galbraith cited by Professor Friedman, there is a trenchant attack by Professor Scott Gordon of Indiana University in the 1968 *Journal of Political Economy*. Professor Gordon wrote as though he were a member of a long-tormented profession who could at last stand it no longer and turned on the persecutor. His sharply-worded assault was not only on the content of Professor Galbraith's writings in the 15 years since 1952 but also on their manner. It was entitled 'The Close of the Galbraithian System' on the ground that 'Galbraith's work will not be the foundation of a new school of economics and . . . its impact on social thought in general is unlikely to outlast the immediate consciousness of the author's contemporaries'. For a writer whose prose style is generally lively and assertive, Professor Galbraith's reply was uncharacteristically muted, restrained and even defensive; and his complaint that Professor Gordon had over-simplified the argument was an echo of the criticisms made of his own writings. Its generally sober tone was similar to that of his reply to Professor Solow (panel, pp. 26-27), described by the latter as 'solemn'. Students of economics and others who have reason to study Professor Galbraith's writings addressed to a wider audience of non-economists should know of his exchanges with his peers.

There were also two further commentaries, by Professor J. E. Meade in the *Economic Journal* (panel, pp. 28-29) and by Mr Robin Marris in the *American Economic Review*, both of whom share some of Professor Galbraith's sympathies and approach but who found fault with his economic analysis.

It would seem that economists who have examined Professor Galbraith's work, and tested his claims against experience, do not share the uncritical awe of the layman in Britain for Galbraithian thinking. The exchanges also show him more sensitive to criticism from his peers than the generally aggressive flavour of his sallies against them for a quarter of a century might have led his readers to suppose.

Professor Galbraith deals mainly with variations of 'market failure' on the side of demand ('private affluence and public squalor', etc.) or supply ('the military-industrial complex', etc.). Even the notion of 'countervailing power' describes an uneasy, unstable confrontation of two large bargainers. Without comparable analysis of 'government failure' his conclusions for government action to improve on imperfect markets are inconclusive and unconvincing. Evidence that markets are imperfect does not create a case for government action, which may be even more imperfect. His 1974 book, *Economics and the Public Purpose,* again relied on examples at random with no effort to show the extent of reality of the claims, assertions, over-simplifications and over-generalisations alleged by fellow-economists. There was still the preference for metaphor over measurement.

Political scientists and sociologists, at least in Britain, who urge the use of government have neglected its imperfections even more than economists, whom Professor Galbraith denounces, have neglected the imperfections of the market. Government failure has been emphasised in the newer economic theories of public choice, of democracy and of bureaucracy, analysed in the past 10 to 15 years by Professors J. M. Buchanan and Gordon Tullock of Virginia, Professor Mancur Olson of the University of Maryland, Professor W. A. Niskanen of the University of California at Los Angeles, Professor E. G. West of Carleton University, Canada, Professor C. K. Rowley of Newcastle University and Professor A. T. Peacock of York University, and several more. It remains to be seen whether in his 1977 BBC lectures Professor Galbraith, who has more experience of government than of industry, will enlighten his British viewers and listeners on the imperfections of government as well as of the market.

Professor Friedman goes further and tries to explain the tenacity with which Professor Galbraith holds to his hypotheses despite the lack of evidence in their support. He argues that essentially the explanation is that Professor Galbraith is a paternalist who believes he knows better than other people how the world should be run and would like to see it run as he thinks best. An alternative explanation for the influence of Professor Galbraith with non-economists is that he enables them to express their distaste for the disagreeable message of the economist that man's most noble instincts cannot all be satisfied simultaneously.

Economists have the unenviable task of telling people confronted with inadequacy that, in a world of resources that are scarce, there are limits to the demands that can be made on them; that man as an individual, firms as units of industry, and governments have to make choices in which they must reject claims that are seen by men of sensibility and compassion as humanitarian. By rejecting 'the conventional wisdom' and poking gentle (or acid) fun at economists, Professor Galbraith has enabled such compassionate consciences to be salved.

The influence of Professor Galbraith in Britain is not easy to explain. His wit and talent for coining memorable phrases may commend themselves to the communications media which look for entertainment to flavour their enlightenment. Professor Galbraith may be one of the best-known economists to non-economists, but he has made very little impact on economics or on his fellow-economists. That has not deterred the BBC from awarding him pride of place in the opportunities they have given to American economists, or indeed to British economists, to explain to the general public what economists are saying that can elucidate the economic world to them. In 1966 he delivered the Reith lectures; he has now been invited to give 13 broadcasts in 1977. This idiosyncratic preference may, perhaps, be explained by the inability of the BBC to judge the sources of the most enduring economic thinking. The economists whom it has chosen to explain economics have generally been the more articulate and the more fashionable, rather than the more profound and the more scholarly. This general failure of the British press and broadcasting to identify the most significant economic thinkers is an element in the impressive critique of British television by Messrs John Birt and Peter Jay[1] that it has been concerned with the ephemeral or superficial rather than the fundamental or profound.

More surprising is the attention lavished on Professor Galbraith by British centres of learning. Trinity College, Cambridge, headed by Lord Butler, elected him a Fellow for the academic year 1970-71; yet it has ignored other economists, American and British, whose contribution to economics is recognised by fellow-economists of all schools as more significant.

The second part of the *Occasional Paper* is based on a talk in

[1] *The Times*, 28 February, 28 September, 1 October, 1975, 2 and 3 September, 1976.

which Professor Friedman discussed the steps that it might be necessary to take to pass from a partial state economy to a freer economy. Here he argued that the immediate financial task was to reduce the rate of inflation in the British economy by shock treatment, modified over 3 to 5 years, rather than by long-term gradual stages. He argued for reduction in government spending not by selective measures but by cuts extending over all departments on the ground that selective cuts would be more likely to generate sectional resistance; a general reduction would induce the interests to contend with one another within the generally reduced total. The second method was to reorganise the tax system by indexing and to reduce its total weight. Here he argued that lower tax rates might yield more revenue. The third task was to denationalise economic activity, again not piecemeal but on a wide scale by auctioning state industries in the market, or by a mutual fund. More gradual measures were required where it was necessary to detach people and industry from dependence on government. Professor Friedman's main proposal was to replace social benefits by vouchers or cash to enable people to pay for formerly 'free' services, buttressed by a negative (in Britain reverse) income tax. He argued the voucher had the two main advantages that it introduced choice and restored competition. A further advantage was that it would make easier the transfer of activity from the government to the individual in the market. And this in turn would make possible a reduction in the weight of the bureaucracy.

Professor Friedman refined some of his argument in the course of replying to questions. Most of the questions centred on the use of the voucher as a technique for introducing choice and competition. He rebutted the view that the voucher would require additional government expenditure in order to cover the small private sector in education (and health) by arguing that its value should be calculated by including all recipients of the service. He thought that the scale of the improvement would be such that the imperfections of experimentation should be risked. And he refuted objections that vouchers could be used by politicians to buy electoral support by the argument that they would create an interest in favour of activity outside the state. His reply here reflected the analysis of 'the vote motive' in the *Hobart Paperback* of that name by Professor Gordon Tullock and Dr Morris

Perlman. The vote motive, he maintained, could be undermined in the last resort only by limiting the scope of government.

As always with Professor Friedman, his writing and thinking will stimulate those inclined to differ as well as those who are persuaded by his analysis and advocacy. The Institute has been inviting him to lecture in Britain since it believes that his work on monetary and social policy has been more perceptive and illuminating than that of other economists who have attracted more attention from the media. Without necessarily sharing his analysis in all particulars, it offers British readers his latest thoughts on the restructuring of the British economy to yield higher output and the advantages that could flow from it.

October/December 1976 ARTHUR SELDON

The Author

MILTON FRIEDMAN was born in 1912 in New York City and graduated from Rutgers before taking his MA at Chicago and PhD at Columbia. From 1935-37 he worked for the US National Resources Committee, from 1937-40 for the National Bureau of Economic Research, and from 1941-43 for the US Treasury.

Since 1946 Friedman has taught at the University of Chicago, where he is now the Paul Snowden Russell Distinguished Service Professor of Economics. He has taught also at the universities of Minnesota, Wisconsin, and Columbia, as well as lecturing at universities throughout the world from Cambridge to Tokyo. Since 1946 he has also been on the research staff of the National Bureau of Economic Research, and, from December 1976, a Senior Research Fellow at the Hoover Institution of Stanford University.

He is known to a wider audience as an advocate of a volunteer army (in place of the US draft), reverse income tax (in place of partial or universalist poverty programmes), monetary policy and floating exchange rates. He is the acknowledged head of the 'Chicago School' which specialises in the empirical testing of policy propositions derived from market analysis. Professor Friedman was awarded the 1976 Nobel Prize in Economic Sciences.

Among his best known books are *Essays in Positive Economics* (Chicago, 1953), *Studies in the Quantity Theory of Money* (edited by Friedman, Chicago, 1956), *A Theory of the Consumption Function* (Princeton, 1957), *Capitalism and Freedom* (Chicago, 1962), (with Anna J. Schwartz) *A Monetary History of the United States, 1867-1960* (Princeton, 1963), and *The Optimum Quantity of Money* (Aldine, Chicago, and Macmillan, London, 1969). The IEA has published his Wincott Memorial Lecture, *The Counter-Revolution in Monetary Theory* (Occasional Paper 33, 1970, 3rd impression 1974), *Monetary Correction* (Occasional Paper 41, 2nd impression 1974), his contributions to *Inflation: Causes, Consequences, Cures* (IEA Readings No. 14, 1974, 2nd impression 1975), and *Unemployment versus Inflation?: An Evaluation of the Phillips Curve* (Occasional Paper 44, 2nd impression 1975).

PART I

The Conventional Wisdom of J. K. Galbraith

I

Introduction

I WANT to start out by explaining that I have no prejudice against John Kenneth Galbraith. Indeed some of my best friends are Galbraithians, including John Kenneth. I say this because there is often somewhat of a tendency to attribute to motives what is really to be attributed to honest difference of opinion. Galbraith deserves a good deal of credit for his independence of mind, for his diligence in trying to spread and promote his ideas, and for an attempt to put intellectual content into some of them.

I mean that seriously. For example, in one policy which is rather peripheral to his general body of thought, namely that of price and wage control, Kenneth Galbraith has the company of many other people from many other points of view who are in favour of, or have from time to time espoused, wage and price control, but so far as I know, he is the only person who has made a serious attempt to present a theoretical analysis to justify his position, in a book called *A Theory of Price Control*[1] he wrote not long after World War II. I happen to think that the analysis is wrong, but at least it is a serious attempt to provide a basis for a point of view.

There are even some subjects and some issues on which he and I have been in agreement. The most important of those, I think, in the United States setting, was the question of military conscription. Kenneth Galbraith, like me, was for many years a strong and public opponent of military conscription, and this despite that some of his closest political allies – for example, Senator Edward Kennedy – were on the other side of the argument. Also, not quite two years ago, when shortly after he became President, Mr Ford assembled a summit meeting of various groups of people to advise him on inflation, I was fascinated to find that at a meeting of economists Galbraith was one of the few outside of

[1] Harvard University Press, Cambridge, Mass., 1952.

those whom you would expect to take this position – the so-called 'liberal' economists – to take the problem of inflation seriously and to regard it as something which had to be corrected.

II

Conviction and Documentation

Having said this, I want to proceed to analyse his thought and his position, but I do so, as I say, with full respect for him as an individual and for his independence. The puzzle I find on reading Galbraith, and the one which will provide something of a theme for what I have to say, is how to reconcile his own sincere *conviction* in the validity of his view of the world with the almost complete failure of any other students – even those who are sympathetic with his general political orientation – to *document* its validity. There have been many people who have looked at his picture of the world, but, although there must be some exceptions, I do not know of any serious scholars who have validated his conception. Kenneth Galbraith has obviously read these criticisms and seen these arguments. The puzzle I want to propose for you is how to reconcile his conviction in the validity of that view with the failure of others to document it.

Affluence for whom?

The typical conventional approach to the conventional wisdom of John Kenneth Galbraith has been to treat him as if he were trying to examine and describe the world and then to compare the position he arrives at with reality. In briefly surveying this conventional approach we may start with *The Affluent Society*,[1] a book, interestingly enough, which was published just before the 'war on poverty' became a widespread obsession. Now I may say I regard that as less of a reflection on Galbraith than on the proponents of the war on poverty. In the fundamental point of view that we are indeed a relatively affluent society, Galbraith was entirely correct. The war on poverty of which so much has been made since then has been a very good thing indeed for many thousands of civil servants who have been able to make excellent careers and many thousands of academic people who have been able to do study after study on poverty. But it has not done very

[1] Hamish Hamilton, 1958; Pelican Books, 1962.

much to help the people who are most disadvantaged in our economy and society.

The main content of the book was not really the affluence of society. Rather it was devoted to other themes: to denigrating the tastes of ordinary people, the tastes of those who prefer pushpin to poetry, who prefer large tailfins to nice, compact, expensive little cars. It was directed to developing the advantages of extending the power of government. A major theme was the alleged contrast between private affluence and public squalor.

In mentioning the criticisms which were made of that theme I must make a start with a review of Galbraith's 1958 *Affluent Society* written by Adam Smith in 1776. I quote from Adam Smith:

> 'It is the highest impertinence and presumption in kings and ministers to pretend to watch over the economy of private people and to restrain their expense either by sumptuary laws or by prohibiting the importation of foreign luxuries. They are themselves always and without any exception the greatest spendthrifts in the society. Let them look well after their own expenses and they may safely trust private people with theirs. If their own extravagance does not ruin the state, that of their subjects never will.'

So I think most of us would agree that 'public affluence and private penury' comes closer to a correct description of the world. I cannot resist adding another of Smith's devastating comments, not so immediately relevant to Galbraith's book but it is a little.

> 'There is no art which one government sooner learns of another than that of draining money from the pockets of the people.'

That is an art which certainly your government and my government have learned very well.

The general reaction of his contemporaries was not much different from Adam Smith's reaction. There was widespread criticism of Galbraith's denigration of public attitudes in terms of his being a 'tailfin burner', like the book burner of an earlier day. Who was he to tell people what they should like?

Galbraith and advertising

There was an examination of his animadversions on advertising. You will recall that one of the main themes in *The Affluent Society* was the enormous power which Galbraith assigned to advertising: that these tastes for tailfins were not natural or native, that they were created by greedy producers seeking to shape the tastes of the public to satisfy their own interests. There resulted a considerable expansion in the economic analysis of advertising which tended to demonstrate, first, that a very large fraction of all advertising was informative rather than persuasive, secondly, that even in persuasive advertising the smart and intelligent thing for an enterprise to do was to find out what the public wants and then make it and advise them of it, not to try to shape its tastes. But, more important from Galbraith's general point of view, there was a great deal of emphasis on the extent to which you had advertising not only by private enterprise but also by government and bureaucrats, and that this has at least as widespread an effect as private advertising.

The statistics on government spending made Galbraith's theme of private affluence versus public squalor an absurd claim. Anybody who studies the statistics knows that government spending has grown apace. In the United States it has grown from about 10 per cent of the national income in 1929 to something over 40 per cent today. In the United Kingdom it has grown from 10 per cent of the national income at the time of the Diamond Jubilee of Queen Victoria to something like 60 per cent today. It is very hard, in the face of these figures, to maintain the claim that it is the private spendthrifts and not the public spendthrifts who are impoverishing the nation.

Countervailing power – the 'unholy trinity'?

Let me go on from his affluent society to his theory of countervailing power,[1] a book to which George Stigler once addressed a devastating review under the title 'The Economist Plays with Blocs'.[2] The thesis which Galbraith set up in that book was that when concentrations of power arise they stimulate countervailing concentrations of power. Big business stimulates big labour, and both stimulate big government. And the combination of big business, big labour and big government is a holy, not an unholy, trinity.

[1] Published under the title *American Capitalism: Concept of Countervailing Power,* Hamish Hamilton, 1952.

[2] *American Economic Review, Papers and Proceedings,* May 1954, pp. 7-14.

The answer to this thesis given by George Stigler and by other critics has been that it is a mistake to suppose that these concentrated groups are always on *different* sides. After all, big business and big labour have *common* interests *vis-a-vis* the consumer. It will be in the self-interest of both groups to operate together to exploit the consumer. In any event, far from this being a countervailing power, or a power that would restore stability and offset the harm done by large conglomerations, it intensifies the harm. Cartel agreements are unstable; and agreements among bilateral or multilateral monopolists are unstable. In any case, the whole Galbraithian argument is factually incorrect. The evidence is that some of the *largest* concentrations of union power are in industries in which the employers have very *little* concentration of power. In the United States, for example, the coal miners' is a major concentrated union, able to gain advantages for its members by acting as a monopolising agent for the industry because the industry itself is so *dispersed*. The coal miners in effect run a cartel on behalf of the employers. Similarly, the teamsters' union, certainly one of the strongest in the United States, did not arise as a countervailing power to some pre-existing corporate monopoly. It arose in part because there was *dispersed* power from which it was able to benefit.

Whither the 'new industrial state'?

This theme of countervailing power is one to which Kenneth Galbraith has in recent years paid almost no attention. He has largely dropped it by the wayside because he has discovered a more attractive way to approach the same objective. And that is through his most ambitious book, *The New Industrial State,*[1] in which he seeks to bring up to date Thorstein Veblen's *The Engineers and the Price System,*[2] with a good deal of help from James Burnham's *The Managerial Revolution.*[3]

This book implied largely a rejection of the thesis of countervailing power in favour of the thesis that control of society is in the hands of a technical-managerial class, the 'technostructure'. One of Galbraith's great abilities is his ability to seize upon key

[1] Pelican Books, 1969.

[2] Harbinger Books, 1963; Augustus Kelley, New York, 1970.

[3] Indiana University Press, 1960 (reprinted by Greenwood Press, New York, 1972).

words and sell them. He is an advertiser *par excellence!* It has always puzzled me why the commercial advertising industry has not recognised that and taken advantage of his extraordinary quality. 'The affluent society' was one such phrase. 'Countervailing power' was another. Now somehow I would think that if you started out with such a clumsy word as 'technostructure' it would not exactly become a common saying, a household word – yet it seems to have caught on very well indeed! The key theme of *The New Industrial State*, as you all know, is that the economy is dominated by giant concerns in which control is in the hands of the technical-managerial class. These have grown so large that individuals are no longer important as entrepreneurs: stockholders play a purely passive role of approving whatever actions management takes and serve no important entrepreneurial function.

This managerial class, according to Galbraith, has as its chief aim security for itself. And it seems to achieve that security by controlling both those who supply goods and services to the enterprise and those who purchase its product. It seems to control both suppliers and demanders, and it does so, of course, with the aid of government. It establishes an effective coalition with the governmental authorities. And together with government it can secure its own future.

It controls its suppliers by being a monopolistic purchaser, the prime source of demand for their products. It controls the demanders by the use of persuasive advertising. This theme from *The Affluent Society* is one that is central to Galbraith's view throughout this whole series of books. In his view the market plays a very minor role indeed. True, there remain some enterprises such as agriculture, small service trades, and so on, which are essentially competitive enterprises subject to market control and market pressure. But they are a tail that is wagged by the dog of the large corporate giants, which in Galbraith's view typify the modern economy.

This view has also been examined and attacked by many scholars. John Jewkes, in his book on *The Sources of Invention*,[1] examines Galbraith's claim that the day of the small enterpriser

[1] [Written with David Sawers and Richard Stillerman, Macmillan, London, 1959 (2nd Edition 1969). Further extracts are added in the panel at pp.18-19. – ED.]

Professor Jewkes on

Professor John Jewkes is an economic authority on the structure of British industry. He was Professor of Economic Organisation at Oxford from 1948 to 1969, Stanley Jevons Professor of Political Economy at Manchester University, 1946-48, Professor of Social Economics at Manchester, 1936-46. He was the Director of the Economic Section of the War Cabinet Secretariat, 1941, and served in other government departments during the war. He has been a member of Royal Commissions.

In *The Sources of Invention* (Macmillan, 1959, 2nd Edition 1969), written with David Sawers and Richard Stillerman, Professor Jewkes quotes Professor Galbraith:

'A benign Providence . . . has made the modern industry of a few large firms an almost perfect instrument for inducing technical change . . . There is no more pleasant fiction than that technical change is the product of the matchless ingenuity of the small man forced by competition to employ his wits to better his neighbour. Unhappily, it is a fiction. Technical development has long since become the preserve of the scientist and the engineer. Most of the cheap and simple inventions have, to put it bluntly, been made.' (*American Capitalism,* p. 91)

Professor Jewkes comments:

Among economists, perhaps no one has exercised more influence than Professor Galbraith with [this] statement . . .
. . . nearly all the systematic evidence has run counter to any such doctrine. Yet, so far as we are aware, Professor Galbraith has said nothing in defence, or in modification, of his views. In his latest book, *The New Industrial State,* he merely repeats his unfounded assertions and dogmatically dismisses anyone who presumes to differ from him:

'It is a commonplace of modern technology that there is a high measure of certainty that problems have solutions before there is knowledge of how they are to be solved.' (p. 19)

is past, that, in Galbraith's words as quoted by Jewkes, 'a benign providence has made the modern industry of a few large firms an almost perfect instrument for inducing technical change'. Jewkes examines this claim and writes at the close of his book:

> 'Nearly all the systematic evidence has run counter to any such doctrine. Yet, so far as we are aware, Professor Galbraith has said nothing in defence, or in modification, of his views'.[1]

[1] *Ibid.*, p. 227.

Professor Galbraith

'Technology, under all circumstances, leads to planning; in its higher manifestations it may put the problems of planning beyond the reach of the industrial firm. Technological compulsions . . . will require the firm to seek the help and protection of the state.' (p. 20)

'By all but the pathologically romantic, it is now recognised that this is not the age of the small man.' (p. 32)

Professor Jewkes and his co-authors also query the contention that the possession of monopoly powers will be an active stimulant to research:

'There must be some element of monopoly in an industry if it is to be progressive.' *(American Capitalism,* p. 23)

They reply:

The general impression left by qualitative inquiries . . . is that for the very slightly concentrated industries (say those where the three largest firms account for 20 per cent or less of the total output) interest in research has been slight and technical advance slow, but that in industries with a higher degree of concentration than this the conditions vary greatly . . .

In view of these inconclusive results it may well be asked how the idea of a close connection between oligopoly and innovation has arisen. Perhaps the most forthright assertions on the subject have been made by Professor Galbraith. *(American Capitalism,* pp. 96-98) He seeks to clinch his argument by comparing the oil industry – oligopolistic and progressive – with the bituminous coal-mining industry – competitive and backward. But the illustration is an unfortunate one for his case. For in the oil industry many of the outstanding ideas have come from outside the industry or from smaller firms. *(The Sources of Invention.* pp. 235-237: the catalytic cracking of petroleum.) As for the bituminous coal-mining industry, it may be technically backward in the United States under competitive conditions, but it is probably even more backward in Great Britain under monopolistic conditions.

Lack of realism and understanding

The validity of Galbraith's picture of the industrial world was attacked from a very different point of view by Sir Frank McFadzean, who is sitting here in the audience and so can correct me if I misrepresent his critique. Sir Frank attacked Galbraith for a lack of realism, and misunderstanding of how large enterprises are run. He attacked the realism of Galbraith's view from the inside, as it were, and demonstrated, I think rather conclusively

Professor McFadzean on

Extracts from F. S. McFadzean, *Galbraith and the Planners*, Strathclyde University Press, 1968.

His analysis quite rightly stresses the importance of the time element in production – the 3½ years that elapsed between the decision to produce the Mustang and the appearance of the first model . . . But [it] is of equal importance in any analysis of . . . maximum profitability and the market. Indeed, without it these words are largely meaningless . . . the Shell Group . . . could increase the return on [its] capital very quickly by cutting out exploration altogether but this would be at the expense of the long-run viability of the Group . . . they behave on the basis that there is a future . . .

Galbraith's statement that the objective of the technostructure is not maximum profitability but the level necessary to keep the shareholders from interefering in the business and provide sufficient capital for expansion, discloses a remarkable naivety as to how a business really operates . . . The corporate planners in Galbraith's unreal world start off with a predetermined level of profit to meet the objectives he postulates and, presumably, juggle with proceeds, volumes, costs and investment to achieve the figure. No planner in the Shell Group – and the same is probably true of other large corporations – would present a forward picture on this basis. It implies a control of events and markets which exists only in a monopoly situation and the imagination of Professor Galbraith.

Where there is competition profit is a residual; it is the result of a vast and complicated series of inter-relationships of proceeds, volume

in a lecture he gave some 10 years ago,[1] that the notion that somehow or other large enterprises were run by faceless impersonal committees with the ability to control their future was a fairy-tale rather than an accurate description.

Galbraith was similarly attacked by Professor G. C. Allen in an excellent *Paper*[2] published by the Institute of Economic Affairs, on similar grounds, but with rather more attention to the behaviour of aggregates, such as industry as a whole, than to the behaviour of particular enterprises. Finally, some studies have been made by an American economist, Harold Demsetz, formerly at the

[1] [*Galbraith and the Planners*, Strathclyde University Press, 1968. Short extracts are added in the panel on this page and p. 21. – ED.]

[2] [*Economic Fact and Fantasy: A rejoinder to Galbraith's Reith Lectures*, Occasional Paper 14, IEA, 1967 (Second Edition 1969). Brief extracts are added in the panel at pp. 22-23. – ED].

Professor Galbraith

> and costs over a period of time and all of these factors contain a wide range of uncertainty . . . over the years, none of our forecasts has been right but our largest errors have usually been in prices.

Professor McFadzean quotes the failure of Ford's Edsel car in the US, the success of Japanese car manufacturers there, and the fluctuating fortunes of the American Motor Corporation. He goes on:

> . . . the British Motor Corporation has singularly failed to perform in Galbraithian terms . . . No amount of reaching forward to bend the consumer to the will of the technostructure prevented the slide . . . After the last war, targets of 220m. tons per annum of coal were bandied around freely. Now, with the rise of cheaper and more convenient fuels, no amount of reaching forward by the techno-structure of the Coal Board is going to prevent a substantial decline in output.
>
> The majority [of companies], large and small, entrepreneurial and mature, normally show profits. Only nationalised industries which, for too long in this country, enjoyed open-ended access to the public purse, can show persistent losses and survive . . .
>
> Professor Galbraith's leap from the rather trite observation that corporations usually make profits to his sweeping generalisations on motivation and the ability of the larger units in the economy to insulate themselves from 'the market' and make a pre-determined level of profit, cannot be justified by any objective analysis.

University of Chicago but currently at the University of California at Los Angeles; he tested three of the Galbraithian hypotheses statistically to see whether the facts coincided with them. Galbraith had emphasised that defence industries were the examples *par excellence* of industries that were capable of controlling their own destinies because they had the government for a client and could effectively control the demand for their products, the prices at which they sold, and the like. Demsetz proceeded to examine the evidence.[1] He examined the market behaviour of the stocks of 13 large defence-oriented industries in the United States. Lo and behold, he found that the real return from investing in those stocks was much more variable from year to year than

[1] ['Economics in the Industrial State—Discussion', *American Economic Review,* May 1970. A short extract is included as the second part of the panel at p. 25. – ED.]

Professor Allen on

Professor G. C. Allen is an authority on the structure of industry. He was Professor of Political Economy at University College, London, 1947-1967, now Emeritus Professor of the University of London. He was a member of the Monopolies Commission, 1950-1962. In 1967 he wrote, for the IEA, *Economic Fact and Fantasy*, sub-titled 'A Rejoinder to Galbraith's Reith Lectures'. When it was reprinted in 1969 he added a postscript commenting on *The New Industrial State*.

In the first edition of *Economic Fact and Fantasy* Professor Allen said:

. . . a controversialist is never justified in presenting an idiosyncratic interpretation of orthodox doctrine in order to give force to his own arguments. It is not permissible to set up Aunt Sallies. Professor Galbraith's expository methods at times violated this principle, and in consequence his lectures, while full of interest and fire, were at some points misleading. (p. 5)

. . . he put forward as if they were novel and heretical various propositions about industrial society which have been accepted as commonplaces by many economists for several decades. (pp. 5-6)

. . . his assertions about the relations of modern industrial concerns to the market are so sweeping and extreme as to render them invalid. (p. 11)

. . . the very diverse profit experience of [large] companies during the last decade . . . certainly lends no support to the implication in Galbraith's argument that [they] enjoy such a well-entrenched position that they can earn a continuous and steady flow of profits. (p. 19)

The notion that the economic history of modern times shows a steady progression from highly competitive markets to monopoly is remote from the truth. (p. 21)

. . . in the face of . . . vast changes in the structure of demand and production, it cannot be asserted that the consumer has been content passively to accept what producers have preferred to give him . . . many of the changes occurred in spite of the entrenched positions of powerful, established firms. (p. 24)

. . . in practice the boards [of nationalised industries] have [not] escaped interference from the executive arm of government. Professor Galbraith, who is usually quick to detect gaps between theory and

the average of all other stocks! It may have been necessary at that time to go to the stock market, but one need merely today observe the fate of some of the defence giants in the United States like Lockheed, General Dynamic and the like, to recognise that they are very, very far indeed from being in a position to control their own destiny. And not even very large expenditures on persuasive advertising in foreign countries enables them to do so.

practice, did not point out this chasm to us. (pp. 27-28)
. . . contrary to Galbraith's assertions about large undertakings in general, public enterprise shares with private enterprise a vulnerability to change . . . the lavish subventions . . . to the railway transport and coal industries have failed to avert a shrinkage. (p. 29)
. . . his analysis of the changes [in Western industrial economies] has been marred by dogmatic and even intemperate assertions. (p. 30)
Throughout his lectures Galbraith argued as if the trends he selected for examination existed in isolation in modern industrial societies and, by ignoring contrary or opposing trends that are also present in them, he reached strongly biassed conclusions. (pp. 30-31)

In the second edition Professor Allen said:

. . . while the efforts made to destroy the market have certainly distorted the way it functions, the forces of competition have continued vigorously to assert themselves, to the dismay of those who think they can be ignored. (p. 34)
[On the effectiveness of government planning, prices and incomes policies, etc.] The evidence of events, in contrast to intentions, does not seem to support Galbraith. (p. 35)
. . . the results [of planning by government and the giant public and private corporations] are a challenge to Professor Galbraith's notion that a great corporation possesses the power to mould demand into conformity with its production plans. (p. 36)

* * *

Professor Allen returned to his critique in *Der Streit um die Gesellschaftsordnung*, Schultless Polygraphischer Verlag, Zurich, 1975, to which he contributed a paper based on a lecture entitled 'A Critical Appraisal of Galbraith's Thinking':

. . . Galbraith has undoubtedly made an original and important contribution to the understanding of modern industrial society. But . . . many of his propositions cannot be accepted without qualification. The industrial system is much more complicated and intricate than it appears in his vision of it. And the solution of the problems created by economic growth and advanced technology cannot be found within the confines of his own ideology.

'No evidence'

Professor Demsetz also examined two other hypotheses of Galbraith's. You would find his article[1] extremely interesting because he points out how difficult it is to get testable hypotheses

[1] ['Where is the New Industrial State?', *Economic Inquiry* (Journal of the Western Economics Association), March 1974. Short extracts are reproduced in the panel at pp. 24-25. – ED.]

Professor Demsetz on

Professor Harold Demsetz, Professor of Economics, University of California at Los Angeles (UCLA) has, in the tradition of the Chicago School of Economics where he previously taught, tested two of Professor Galbraith's central hypotheses on the structure of industry (that the goals of the 'technostructure' are stability and sales maximisation) by measuring the performance of 375 industries.

He writes ('Where is the New Industrial State?', *Economic Inquiry*, USA, March 1974):

The debate about the new industrial state has been carried on at three levels. First, the sensibleness of the reports brought back by the only living authority on the whereabouts of the new state has been examined in several reviews of Galbraith's works. Secondly, the epistemology of Galbraith's discoveries has been examined, and special note has been taken of the similarity between his reports and those of his teacher, Thorstein Veblen. And, thirdly, Galbraith's sermons on how best to reorganise this new state have been questioned. . . . very little effort has been devoted to the task of ascertaining whether the new industrial state actually exists. There is good reason for this since Galbraith's lively prose seldom allows its author a cleanly stated testable hypothesis. The technostructure of the new industrial state seeks nothing less than the 'panoply of organisation interests – security and autonomy of organisation, growth – technical achievement, public prestige, as well as profits'. ('Economics as a System of Belief', *American Economic Review*, 1970.) Anyone wishing to validate Galbraith's discovery is forced to cull specific hypotheses from his ranging rhetoric . . . the present paper discuss[es] the results of a serious search for that fabled and very well advertised land, the new industrial state.

There does exist in Galbraith's work one concisely stated hypothesis. Perhaps this exception to Galbraith's style is due to the origin of the hypothesis, which, as Galbraith acknowledges, is attributable to others, such as William J. Baumol. This hypothesis states that techno-structure-oriented firms sacrifice profits in order to accelerate growth of sales . . .

out of the Galbraithian canon. Galbraith speaks in broad general terms; he makes assertions about the world at large. But they are very seldom put in a form in which they yield testable hypotheses. In addition to the one about defence industries, Demsetz tested, through multiple correlation of the experience of many enterprises, the Galbraithian theme that technostructure-oriented

Professor Galbraith

A second hypothesis . . . is the desire of various echelons of management to prevent the disruption of the firm's plans. This hypothesis is more purely Galbraithian, and also is considerably less concise. The problem that instability creates for the fulfillment of plans is discussed in *The New Industrial State*. (p. 17)

. . . to assess the validity of these two doctrines about how the management of the modern corporation behaves . . . it is necessary to measure the degree to which firms or industries achieve these two managerial goals in comparison with the degree to which these firms or industries are likely to be guided by the imperatives of modern technology. Galbraith never instructs his readers explicitly as to a method by which it can be ascertained which firms are most closely bound by the demands of modern technology. But some guidance can be found in a close reading of Galbraith which indicates that the following characteristics identify firms that are technostructure oriented – capital intensive production methods, extensive use of advertising, oligopolistic industry structure, large firm size, and orientation toward military production.

* * *

The only conclusion permitted by [my] investigation is that Galbraith's notions are remarkably consistent in their inability to find confirmation. These negative results confirm other testing of Galbraith's views that I presented at the 1969 meetings of the American Economic Association . . .

I analysed a sample of defence stocks . . . The sample contained 13 of the top prime defence contractors for whom defence contracts accounted for over 30 per cent of sales. These stocks over the period 1949-64 offered to investors about 21 per cent *more* risk, measured by fluctuations in year-to-year rates of return to shareholders, than did randomly selected portfolios of 13 stocks per portfolio.

The evidence that I have been able to uncover reveals that Galbraith's work possesses to a remarkable degree one of the essential attributes of successful science – consistency. Consistency, however, is not enough. Columbus had a great deal more corroboration for his belief that he found the Indies than Galbraith has for his discovery of the new industrial state.

firms sacrifice profits to accelerate the growth of sales. Galbraith's theme here is that once you get one of these large corporations with the technocrats in the technostructure in command, they have to have certain minimal profits in order to satisfy the stockholders and keep them quiet, but beyond that what they really want to do is to grow. And so, argues Galbraith, they are willing

Professor Solow on

In 'The New Industrial State, or Son of Affluence' (*The Public Interest,* Fall 1967) Professor R. M. Solow of the Massachusetts Institute of Technology shows sympathy with Professor Galbraith's general philosophic outlook but makes criticisms of economic substance.

Professor Galbraith is not the first person to have discovered General Motors. Most close students of industrial investment or pricing do make room in their statistical behaviour equations for behaviour that is neither perfectly competitive nor simply monopolistic. (p. 103)

The economic system conforms neither to Galbraith's nor to any other simple model:

... it is unlikely that the economic system can usefully be described either as General Motors writ larger or as the family farm writ everywhere. (p. 103)

The sphere of large corporate enterprise does not constitute the whole economy:

There is . . . a moderate amount of economic activity that is not carried on by . . . the 100 largest or 500 largest corporations . . . The giant corporation is pre-eminently a phenomenon of manufacturing industry and public utilities; it plays a much less important role in trade and services. If, as seems to be in the cards, the trade and service sectors grow relative to the total, the scope of the large corporation may be limited. (p. 103)

to sacrifice profits for the sake of sales. Demsetz proceeded to assemble data on firms and to classify them as technostructure-oriented by the kind of criteria Galbraith used. He then tried to see whether it was true that there was a trade-off of profits against sales. *He could find no evidence for it whatsoever.*

He also investigated Galbraith's thesis that such firms use the control of prices, of advertising and of government intervention to prevent the disruption of their plans. Again he did this by trying to see whether firms of that type in practice have more stable income and profits than other firms. Again he found no confirmation at all of this Galbraithian claim.

Misinterpretation of economic theory and research

There have been many other criticisms of Galbraith's views, including many by people who are politically very sympathetic to

Professor Galbraith

On the effects of the separation of ownership and control, and of the extent of profit maximisation as the motive of management, Professor Solow says:

It is possible to argue – and many economists probably would argue – that many management-controlled firms are constrained by market forces to behave in much the same way that an owner-controlled firm would behave, and many others acquire owners who like the policy followed by the management . . . it may be a fair complaint that this proposition has not received all the research attention it deserves. It is an error to suppose it has received none at all. Such evidence as there is does not give a very clear-cut answer, but it does not suggest that the orthodox presupposition is terribly wrong. Galbraith does not present any convincing evidence the other way, as I think he is aware. The game of shifting the burden of proof that he plays at the very end of this book [*The New Industrial State*] is a child's game. Economics is supposed to be a search for verifiable truths, not a high-school debate. (pp. 103-104)

And on the extent that the producer can 'manipulate' the consumer, by the use of advertising, Solow argues:

The issue is whether the art of salesmanship has succeeded in freeing the large corporation from the need to meet a market test, giving it 'decisive influence over the revenue it receives'.

That is not an easy question to answer, at least not if you insist on evidence. Professor Galbraith offers none; perhaps that is why he states his conclusion so confidently and so often. (p. 105)

his orientation, such as for example the extremely critical review of *The New Industrial State* by Robert Solow,[1] in which he criticised Galbraith as misinterpreting both economic theory and recent research. The claim that the managers can neglect the stockholders because enterprises are large has itself been subjected to an enormous amount of study. We all know that the stock market exerts an influence in a very indirect but effective way. And, no matter how large the enterprise, if the managers act in such a way as to earn less than is feasible with those resources, this has an effect on the price of the stock. If the stock price is driven down it

[1] [Professor Robert M. Solow's critique, 'The New Industrial State, or Son of Affluence', appeared in *The Public Interest*, No. 9, 1967. Professor Galbraith's reply, in the same issue, was entitled 'A Review of a Review'. Professor Solow responded with 'A Rejoinder'. Extracts from this critique in a journal not widely read in Britain are assembled in the panel at pp. 26-27. Another friendly critic was Professor J. E. Meade (panel, pp. 28-29). – ED.]

Professor Meade on

In 'Is "The New Industrial State" Inevitable?', *(Economic Journal,* June 1968), Professor Meade says:

> ... when one has cast aside all Professor Galbraith's exaggerations there remains a very important core of truth in his assertions. The large modern industrial corporation does cover an important sector of the economy, and its management does call for a new dimension of planning; its control has without question passed from its legal owners to its technostructure, which does not have the same direct interest in maximising profit; the technostructure does attempt through advertisement and other sales techniques to create, mould and control the tastes of individual consumers; and it does have exceptionally close contacts with, and influence over, government programmes for the procurement of complicated industrial products, in particular in connection with armaments. (p. 381)

Professor Meade's criticisms are:

> ... there is a very large part of economic activity which is not controlled by the modern industrial corporation and ... there are very important new developments of governmental policy that are not due to the influence of the technostructure. (p. 381)

While individual large corporations might have considerable 'planning' power, Galbraith

> never explains why and by what mechanism these individual plans can be expected to build up into a coherent whole. (p. 377)

Galbraith confuses the issues by over-simplified conceptions of

provides somebody with an incentive to buy up the stock, engage in take-over activity, and in this way kick out the current management. And there have been enough cases of this occurring for every manager in every major enterprise to recognise where his own self-interest lies.

It is very interesting indeed that the enterprises which come closest, in my opinion, to conforming to Galbraith's picture of the modern giants are some of the *nationalised* industries, because there indeed there is no effective stock market to enforce on the managers the promotion of the interests of the enterprise.

The main purpose of going over this examination of the evidence is that, so far as I know, apart from Galbraith's own assertion, *there has been no successful defence of this view of the world.* That does not mean there are no defenders of the view.

Professor Galbraith

the meaning of 'planning' and the 'market':

> It is by [such] silly contrasts . . . that Professor Galbraith pokes fun at his professional colleagues. (p. 382)

The existence of profit maximisation cannot be denied or replaced in analysis by growth maximisation:

> . . . a high rate of growth depends upon a high rate of profit; and in so far as the technostructure cannot mould at its will the markets in which the company's inputs and outputs are sold, the company's policy which results from the search for growth will closely, though not always exactly, resemble the company's policy which would result from a competitive search for profit. (p. 387)

Large corporations are not invulnerable to competition:

> . . . even large companies are subject to the pressures of potential competition . . . from enterprising small newcomers or from large rivals in other lines of production . . . the technostructure in any large company must continuously search for ways of maintaining its profitability in order to avoid outside threats to its own growth or even to its security. (p. 387)

The consumer is not a puppet, and the failure of such products as (US) Ford's Edsel is not exceptional:

> . . . many other instances of a less dramatic character could be quoted . . . It is really misleading of Professor Galbraith to demote consumers' tastes to such an indecisive role in his explanation of the workings of the modern economy. (p. 383)

There are many. There are many who accept it. But I know of no scientific studies which have validated that view of the world as meaningful and accurate in the sense that it yields predictions about the behaviour of enterprises, of industry, or of the economy as a whole that can be checked, tested against evidence, and found to hold.

III

Galbraith – Scientist or Missionary?

And that brings me back to the puzzle I started with. How can so intelligent, thoughtful and independent a mind as Kenneth Galbraith's hold such an apparently indefensible view of reality? The basis for an answer, I think, is to be found by re-examining

Galbraith's purpose and approach. Instead of regarding him as a scientist seeking explanations, I think we shall get more understanding if we look at him as a missionary seeking converts. We must therefore examine not his evidence, not his hypotheses, but his values and his philosophy, his ideology. If we do so I think we shall see that his view of the world derives from his ideological view, and not the other way round.

Galbraith a Tory Radical?

Galbraith has always seemed to me a 20th-century version of the early 19th-century Tory Radicals of Great Britain. Some of you will have read a book by Cecil Driver called *Tory Radical: The Life of Richard Oastler.*[1] At any rate, there was a group of Tories in the early 19th century called Tory Radicals, whose position was, as I see it, very similar to Galbraith's position today. They believed in an aristocracy, as he does. They knew they were members of that aristocracy, as he does. They had membership in it by virtue of birth; he has membership in it by virtue of other qualities. They believed that the aristocracy had an obligation to the masses and that they were the only disinterested group in the community that could serve the masses, because their position came to them naturally, without effort necessarily on their part, and this provided them with an obligation at the same time that it in large measure assured their disinterestedness. They believed, however, that they should not – and Galbraith believes that he should not – use force to impose their views on the masses. Their approach was fully paternalistic: they were in a position of a father to children, whose children would naturally recognise the superiority of the father and that his values were superior to theirs. And so the Tory Radicals expected, and thought it appropriate, that the masses would accept the dominion of the aristocrats over their values and beliefs, because the aristocrats were seeking their welfare. I believe that Galbraith's view is essentially the same. He is not in favour of any kind of imposition on the masses of the values he stands for. He knows that his values are superior to those of the masses, and he thinks that if the masses are properly instructed by enough of his books, they will come themselves to that view and will ask him and his fellow intellectuals to take charge.

[1] Octagon, New York, 1946 (reprinted 1970).

He has thus always reminded me of the Tory Radicals, but Shirley and William Letwin[1] and others have persuaded me that there is also a strong admixture of John Stuart Mill's philosophical radicalism. I can demonstrate that element most quickly and effectively by reading a few quotations from Maurice Cowling's book on *Mill and Liberalism*.[2] You will see that each of these quotations, which Maurice Cowling regards as applicable to John Stuart Mill, is every bit as applicable to Galbraith.

First:

'. . . "the higher minds" should set the tone of the society in which they live; and hence . . . *their* sort of education in general culture must be propagated as extensively as possible'. (p. 37)

Second:

'. . . Mill's fundamental principles have neither proof nor philosophical authority, but are commitments to action, the outcome of assertions to claim knowledge of the nature of the world and the direction men's duty ought to take within it: . . . it is difficult to avoid feeling that much of what we will characterise as his *arrogance* is connected with want of clarity at this point.' (p. 77)

Note that 'want of clarity' is about whether his assertions have scientific authority.

There is no-one who does not apply the word 'arrogant' to Galbraith, and with justice. It applies precisely for the reason that Cowling refers to it in Mill: because Galbraith treats his assertions as if they have scientific authority, as if they have been demonstrated, when they have not been at all. His principles, as Cowling says about Mill's, are commitments to action.

Third:

'Mill was one of the most censorious of 19th-century moralists. At every turn, denigration of existing society is offered with inquisitorial certainty . . .'. (p. 143)

Finally:

'If a writer believes a doctrine he is promulgating, and feels an obligation to it, he is unlikely to reveal its limitations'. (p. 147)

[1] [William Letwin is Professor of Political Science at the London School of Economics. His wife, Shirley Robin Letwin, has taught, *inter alia*, at the LSE and is the author of *The Pursuit of Certainty*, Cambridge University Press, 1965, and other works. – ED.]

[2] Cambridge University Press, 1963.

Reconciling lack of evidence with dogmatic conviction

That brings me back to my main theme: the reconciliation of the factual inadequacy of the Galbraithian view and the dogmatic confidence with which he asserts it. I want to show how you can link the position he takes about the world with his ideological and philosophical view.

First, Galbraith's Tory Radical position implies that the values of the masses are inferior to those of the intellectual aristocracy, and that, of course, is the theme that runs throughout his analysis. But, moreover, if the values of the masses are created by self-interested advocates in industry, then they have no claim to be considered as valid, or to be respected. Thus, in order for Galbraith to strengthen his emphasis on the right of the aristocracy to shape the values of the masses, it is extremely convenient to be able to treat those values as having no validity but simply as the creation of self-interested advocates.

This has further implications. If it is possible for values to be altered by advertising, Mill's 'higher minds' can affect them too. After all, if these commercial advertisers can shape man's life, there is meaning to having a society in which the higher minds can shape man's wants and values. And you can have some success from this Tory radical political programme of the leading aristocrats, so there is point to having them in power.

Moreover, if you have rule by a free market, if a free market really ruled in response to valid consumer wants, that would provide an alternative to rule by higher minds. It would also render such rule difficult or impossible to achieve. Many reformers – Galbraith is not alone in this – have as their basic objection to a free market that it frustrates them in achieving their reforms, because it enables people to have what they want, not what the reformers want. Hence every reformer has a strong tendency to be adverse to a free market. Galbraith in particular must regard it as trivial or non-existent, or else his whole ideological case, both its justification and its possibility, collapses.

If the free market is not the ruler, who are the rulers? Not, according to Galbraith, entrepreneurs serving the market, but technocrats, who have no moral authority. Besides, they are not disinterested. These technocrats are self-selected, they make their own jobs, they appoint one another. What right do they have to decide people's tastes, or how the resources of a community should be used? If you had Adam Smith entrepreneurs running the society in response to the demands of the public, that would have some moral authority. But the technocrats have no moral authority: they are running it in their own interest.

I believe that this is a very important feature in the Galbraithian view. It serves both to justify his emphasis on rule by the intellectual class and also to enhance its appeal to the public at large. We all want somebody to blame things on. Nothing that happens that is bad is our fault; it's other people who do it to us. And all the better if those other people are faceless bureaucrats in the private sector whom we did not elect, we did not choose. They just somehow got there.

Incidentally, if the technocracy rules, if the technocracy fixes prices and wages for its own convenience, then government officials can do so also. However, as I mentioned earlier, Galbraith's attitude towards price and wage control is not really central to his position. You can subtract it and leave his position unaltered. It is really peripheral to it; it arises out of the sheer accident that he happened to spend part of World War II as a price controller.

This interpretation of Galbraith's view of the world seems to me to make it all of one piece and explains his stubbornness in adhering to it. The characteristics he attributes to the world are essential to upholding his values, his ideological and his political position. But it also explains the grounds on which other people object to it, including myself. The philosophical radicals, like the socialists, attacked the aristocracy. In this they were quite a bit different from Galbraith. On the other hand, they were similar to Galbraith in that insofar as there were to be leaders they wanted them to be a meritocracy rather than an aristocracy. And in this respect Galbraith joins them.

Meritocracy or aristocracy – the lesser evil

I must say I object to being ruled either by the natural-born aristocracy or by a meritocracy but, if I have to be ruled by either, it seems to me that aristocracy of birth is much the lesser evil if only because those who are born to be aristocrats are less likely to be arrogant. They know it is an accident. This was of course the endearing feature of the Tory Radicals, that they recognised they were accidentally in the position of leadership. This is what, in their view, gave them their obligations to the rest of the community, their *noblesse oblige*. But a meritocracy, people who know that they are *abler* than their fellows, and are therefore in a position to rule? Heaven forbid!

More fundamentally, of course, I object to the view that any aristocracy should rule. I believe it is of the utmost arrogance for any of us to suppose that we have the right to decide what is the better and the worse value for others by any means other than persuasion. We may of course have strong views of our own: we may believe very strongly that poetry is better than pushpin, or the reverse. But for those of us who believe in the dignity of the individual human being, in the pre-eminence of freedom among human beings as the objective of social organisation: we must say that the only way in which we have any right to try to affect the values of others is by persuasion. And that, I may say, includes commercial advertising, which I view as a form of free speech and which ought to be just as much subject as other forms of discourse to the First Amendment of the United States Constitution prohibiting governmental measures against free speech. (The US Supreme Court, I am delighted to say, has recently so ruled.)

Galbraith v. Adam Smith

These are, I believe, the fundamental grounds on which the battle is drawn. Throughout all history there have been the superiors who have believed that they have the right to rule the inferiors. And the only method of social and economic organisation that has ever been developed which avoids that result is the method which Adam Smith espoused in his *Wealth of Nations*: voluntary co-operation among individuals in which each man is free to use his own capacities and resources as he wills in accordance with his own values so long as he does not interfere with the right of others to do likewise. That is a view of the world which is profoundly opposed by the Galbraithian view of the world.

Galbraith would not oppose the Adam Smith view explicitly as undesirable; he never does that. He would agree with every word I have just said. But if he were here he would say:

> *'Ah, but you're a visionary. That's unrealistic. That isn't the way the world really is. Technical development and technical growth have made it essential that we have these large corporations*

and these large governments and these large organisations. And therefore your picture is a dream, a Utopia that is incapable of achievement.'

That is a claim which I believe the various critics of Galbraith have shown to be unfounded. These large enterprises are in practice not large relative to the market as a whole, not any larger than they were a hundred years ago. Large governments are not produced, and have not been produced, by technical necessities making things occur on a larger scale. There is no technical necessity arising out of technological development that requires an expansion of welfare programmes, of rent controls, of government housing, of public health. Not one of these reflects technological pressure.

They reflect rather an erroneous approach of trying to use *political* methods to achieve good objectives. The growth of government reflects rather the invisible hand in politics which works in the opposite direction from the invisible hand in economics.

In *economics* those people who attempt to pursue only their own self-interest are led by an invisible hand to promote the *public* interest.

In the *political* sphere individuals like Galbraith who attempt to pursue the public interest as they view it are led by an invisible hand to further *private* interests which it is no part of their intention to promote.

IV

Questions and Answers

Easy (wrong) and difficult (right) economic thinking

QUESTION: I work in the City and the Stock market and I have been in a university for a very long time before. The thing that really puzzles me, and while I agree with most of your views, why is it that the theories and thoughts of Professor Galbraith find so much more of an audience in the academic world than your views? And do you think that there is any change occurring?

FRIEDMAN: The answer to that is they don't. I don't mean to be in any way other than strictly factual. Galbraith's theories have never found any acceptance in the *academic* world – their acceptance has been in the *public* world. He has written for the public at large. Now I will restate your question: Why do his theories find so much more acceptance in the public world than the theories or arguments of persons like myself? And the answer is because they are much more satisfying to the ordinary man. They are easy to understand – it is easy to understand that if something is wrong there's some devil somewhere who's doing it to you. On the other hand, the kind of theories that people like me try to put across are hard to understand. This is a great defect unfortunately; it has always been one of the great difficulties of getting a market system accepted. The argument for a market is a sophisticated argument. It has to do with how a complicated system works indirectly by channels that nobody sees, by forces that have no names attached to them. That is a much harder point of view to get across than the notion that particular people are pulling levers and doing things to you. It is much harder to get across the idea that the way to cure a problem may be to allow the impersonal forces of the market to work than the idea that the way to cure something is to pass a law and appoint a minister. If you have a drought, well, you obviously appoint a Minister of Drought! The only reason why the market system has managed to survive to the extent that it has is because it is so much more efficient and effective than all of these ministers. If it were not, if the market system were not 10 times as efficient as the governmental system, all of our countries would long since have had the market completely taken over.

Let me go back, however, to your first point because I think it is very important and interesting. If someone speaks of the school of Adam Smith you can name people, academic, scientific people who are followers of Smith. If we speak of the Keynesians we can name respectable academics who have contributed to the Keynesian canon and to the Keynesian view. It is very hard to name academic people who have contributed to the Galbraithian view. It's fundamentally a one-man crusade. Go back to the philosophical radicals. That wasn't John Stuart Mill alone; there was quite a group of intellectually respectable people contributing to the argument. Whom else can you name who belongs to the Galbraithians? And I cite this as evidence to support my answer to your question, that you are confusing a popular reaction with an academic and intellectual reaction.

Inflation in Chile

QUESTION: . . . Have the policies of the present government in Chile been successful in curing inflation?

FRIEDMAN: Well, that has very little to do with John Kenneth Galbraith but I'll be glad to answer it. In the first place let me make one point clear. I have not been guiding the economic policies of Chile! I have not known over the past year or so whether to be more flattered or amused by the powers which have been attributed to me. I spent six days a year ago (in April 1975) in Chile and have had no contact since with anybody in Chile and yet I am given credit for guiding the day-to-day policies of that government. But let me say the answer to your question is that, first of all, the government of Chile has not followed a severely deflationary policy; they have reduced the rate of growth of the money supply from something over 20 per cent a month to something in the neighbourhood of 10 per cent a month. Now that's a sharp reduction and that has been accompanied by a reduction in the rate of inflation from something over 20 per cent a month to something under 10 per cent a month. So as I understand it – all of this is secondhand, I have not studied the recent statistics myself, but I have talked with people who are experts on the Chilean situation – the evidence seems to be that there has been a sharp reduction in the rate of inflation as a result of a sharp reduction in the rate of monetary growth; this result followed with a much shorter lag of course than it would here.

As you know, in the United States and the United Kingdom there has over the past hundred years been about a two-year lag between changes in the money supply and changes in prices. That's not a fact of nature, but a result of our both having systems which had relatively stable prices over fairly long periods. In countries like Chile or Brazil or Argentina and the like the lag is much shorter; a change in the money supply is followed within a few months by the appropriate price changes because people have been much more attuned to wide fluctuations in the rate of inflation. Now, as I understand the Chilean situation, the initial relatively deflationary policies did have the expected consequences both of a reduction in the rate of inflation and an initial reduction in output and employment. In addition, the government undertook to cut down government spending, to privatise enterprises, putting them back into private hands, to free foreign exchange.

As I understand it, there has been a very rapid improvement in non-traditional exports and in the foreign balance of payments. I am told that the major source of the increases in the money supply in the past year have come from the necessity of raising funds to pay off foreign debts. The output in agriculture has increased very rapidly in the past two years, industrial output has fallen and industrial unemployment rose in Santiago, but there has been a turn and the indices of production and employment are now going up.

Will Galbraith come true?

QUESTION: Will Galbraith's view be the view of the future?

FRIEDMAN: No. The future may be a technostructure, but if so it will be a government collectivist technostructure and not a private industry technostructure. The great danger of the Galbraithian view is precisely that it stresses the importance, from his point of view, of an expansion in the role of government. Unfortunately, while he would like to see that governmental role be carried through by disinterested intellectuals, it will not be. It will be carried through by very highly interested bureaucrats, and they will run the society from the centre as such societies have always tended to be run: as collectivist societies which reduce and greatly limit the freedom of individuals.

There are two different questions. What is *likely* to happen and what *can* happen; what *needs* to happen, what is *possible*. Many of the large aggregations of enterprise, I would argue, have arisen from bad government policy and not from technological necessity. In my country, about which I can speak much more confidently than I can about yours, our tax system has established a very strong pressure toward merger and conglomeration of enterprises. Governmental control and regulation in industries such as the power industry, the telephone industry, the communications industry, the aircraft industry, have made for large enterprises. The most obvious example is aircraft. Since the Civil Aeronautics Board started to exercise control over air carriers, in the 1930s, not a single new trunk line has been approved, and the number of major trunk lines in the United States is smaller today than it was in 1938. And this is not for want of applicants – there have been many applicants. If we could abolish the Civil Aeronautics Board tomorrow, there is no doubt whatsoever that our aircraft industry would be in an extremely healthy state, with a very much larger number of enterprises and very much less concentration of power. The same is true in the broadcasting and television industry. Why do we have three major networks? Because the Federal Communications Commission has prevented competition in television and radio. It has held back the introduction of pay TV, of cable TV, of every new invention. If we could abolish the Federal Communications Commission tomorrow and auction off the right to the various channels and so on, there is no doubt that in a very short period we would have a much larger number of very effective and efficient television companies. And so it goes in industry after industry.

The relationship between size and government control, in my opinion, is the reverse of that which Galbraith presents. He presents a picture in which the large enterprises grow and then take the government in to help them plan. Now there is no doubt that business enterprises will in fact *try* to use the government for their purposes and often are successful in doing so. Adam Smith wrote that two centuries ago. But the relationship in the United States has been that government measures have promoted the concentration of industry and the growth of large enterprises; and in the absence of the government measures that need not have happened at all. So I don't think there is any necessity for the Galbraithian picture, either for the present or for the future.

But I very much fear that we may develop in the direction of an increasingly bureaucratised, collectivist, socialist kind of society – that is the direction in which Britain is going. If I am an English businessman the sensible thing for me to do is to make large losses, provided I can counterpoise those losses with an accumulation of foreign exchange somewhere. Then the government will come in and bale me out of my losses and buy me out. This is a way in which British industry has been increasingly taken over by your government, which has been borrowing foreign exchange abroad to enable people at home to get their money out. Now it's a good thing that people should be able to get their money out: I am not in favour of exchange control, I think it ought to be abolished, but I'm only describing the process that has been going on and why I think that you're moving in that direction rather than the other direction. It's an interesting thing that one of Galbraith's major points, one on which Sir Frank McFadzean particularly attacked him correctly, was in saying 'Oh, these big enterprises never make losses'. Now you could hardly think of any prophecy which has been more convincingly contradicted by the experience in the United States and Britain.

Motive and consequence in economic policy

QUESTION: What empirical evidence is there for the good intentions of the reformers?

FRIEDMAN: The question is very interesting. I have to admit I have no answer. However, I do not believe it is a crucial point. The important point is a different one.

I said that there was an invisible hand in the political sphere whereby those well-meaning people who attempted to use the political mechanism to do good were led to serve private interests that they would never voluntarily have served. On the whole it seems to me very unsatisfactory to attack issues by trying to question what people's *motives* are. That gets you into a morass. First of all, an argument may be right or wrong regardless of the motives of the person who presented it. The person may have presented a self-interested argument – that does not mean it is wrong. The important question is: What are the *consequences* of the way people behave and act? And the only point I would make is – for the moment let's grant complete disinterest on the part of the people, let's grant the best of intentions. What would be the consequences? And would it really be true that the bad consequences of these measures follow from the bad intentions, or would those bad consequences follow even if people had good intentions? The reply I would give is that even if people had the very best of intentions – and I don't question their motives – the evil consequences that we have seen would still follow. Why?

Economic v. political markets

The reason is the fundamental difference between an economic mechanism and a political mechanism. The fundamental difference is that in the economic market you get what you pay for. In the political market you do not get what you vote for. Now that's a very fundamental difference in its simplest terms. If in the economic market I go to spend a dollar I am going to get a dollar's worth and therefore I have a dollar's worth of incentive to make sure I spend that dollar well. If I go to vote in the political market, at most mine is one of a thousand votes and I'm not going to get what I vote for, I'm going to get what 51 per cent of the people vote for. And therefore in general *I have no incentive to vote intelligently.*

Suppose I am asked to vote on the question of whether there should be a tariff on shoes, or indirectly whether my representative should vote for it. How much money is it worth my spending to inform myself on that issue? The answer is one cent, or two cents. On the other hand, the manufacturers of shoes are in a different situation: their interests are concentrated; that particular measure (the tariff) means a great deal to them. It will be worth their while to spend a good deal getting that measure passed. That is why it is in the political self-interest of people in politics to create and serve a coalition of special interests rather than a general interest. In the same way let people, with the best intentions in the world, legislate a measure. Who has any incentive to keep tabs on what happens to it after it's voted? The public at large is led to believe that poor people are getting cheated in their housing and so they vote for rent control. But once the rent control authority is established, in whose interest is it run? And this goes on over and over again – the Inter-State Commerce Commission, the FDA, whatever you want to name. The political process is one which has an invisible hand in the sense that *it is against the private interest to vote in the public interest.* And therefore *you cannot have a political mechanism which will in practice achieve the sum of the general public interest as the market does.*

I haven't really answered your question – I'm not sure I can – but do let me urge that we will do much better if we don't get ourselves involved in calling names or questioning motives but take people for what they profess to be. After all, we're asking them to do that to us!

One of the great puzzles is how to explain the growth of this kind of intervention. This is the question we started with. And another kind of an answer is that for many of us it is in our self-interest to be in favour of intervention. Certainly for economists, there is nothing that produces jobs for economists like government controls and government intervention. And all economists are therefore schizophrenic: their discipline, derived from Adam Smith, leads them to favour the market; their self-interest leads them to favour intervention. And in large part the profession has been led to reconcile these two opposing forces by being in favour of the market in general but opposed to it in particular. We are very clever at finding 'special cases' – there are external effects, there are monopolies, there are imperfections in the market; therefore we can have our cake and eat it. We can be in favour of the free market and we can at the same time promote those separate interventions that promote our private interest by providing jobs for economists.

PART II

Curing the British Disease: The Steps From Here to There

Before we start on the discussion I cannot resist informing some of you, and Arthur Seldon[1] in particular, that there are some respects in which American trade unions are worse than British trade unions. I have just discovered one this afternoon, in taping a brief comment for the BBC. In the United States if a gentleman like Terence Kelly[2] came around to interview me with a cassette tape recorder and one side of the cassette tape ran out and he had to turn it over, that cassette would be wiped out when he got back to the office because it is the function of a technician, not of a reporter, to turn the cassette over. And so he has to be sure that he can record everything on one side of the cassette! But here in Britain I saw Terence here – and this is a tape recorder rather than a cassette recorder – actually put in a new tape! Now that surely is a job for a technician! Now why is that? Because the trade unions don't think there's enough fat in the BBC to go after? What the reason is, I don't know, but at any rate you'll be glad to know that you've got some advantages.

* * *

We need to divide the major question 'from here to there' into two very different issues. One has to do with the problem of how you get out of the kind of situation in which Britain now is, with something like 60 per cent of the national income being spent by government, and with an inflation which has gone up and down for years. How you turn that situation around and get the basic economic structure of the economy into a healthy situation is one class of problem. There is a second and very different class of

[1] [A reference to a deviation from the monetarist view that trade unions have no direct role in generating inflation. The deviating view is that unions in strong bargaining positions can in Britain induce government to inflate in order to stimulate demand and so avoid the unemployment that would follow monopoly labour costs that cannot be passed on in higher prices. The process is not 'cost-push', but 'politician-push'; the mechanism or instrument of inflation remains the money supply, mismanaged by government monopoly. – ED.]

[2] [The BBC interviewer; he is the producer of the BBC radio programme 'Dateline'. – ED.]

problem: how do you unwind the various social welfare or industrial invervention measures that your government undertakes? The first is a problem of general financial policy and the second of detailed social and economic policy.

I

The Immediate Financial Task

The first of these is in some ways the immediate problem that a country like Britain is faced with. Suppose you had the will, which you haven't, how should you go about trying to get the economy on to a healthy basis?

Gradualism

Now in this particular issue I believe that one major question is gradualism *versus* shock treatment. That is a question to which the same answer cannot be given under all circumstances. If you are in the situation of the United States today, with an inflation rate running at about 6 per cent a year, total governmental spending at about 40 per cent of the national income – in which we have been getting worse but are at a much less advanced state of the disease than you are – I am all in favour of a very gradual return to a non-inflationary position. I would not be in favour of trying to get a zero rate of inflation next year because there are all sorts of contracts people have entered into, including borrowing and lending contracts at rates of interest that implicitly allow for a considerable measure of inflation. There are employment contracts, building contracts, and so on, and it would be very disturbing to the arrangements voluntarily reached amongst individuals if you were overnight to go from, say, 6 per cent to zero. I think in the United States it would be desirable to go to zero over a period of four or five years, by cutting down the rate of inflation by about 1 per cent per year. Personally I would like to see that policy announced in advance so that people could adjust themselves to it. And I would call that a relatively gradual approach to a state of financial equilibrium.

Shock treatment

On the other hand, to take the extreme opposite case: a year ago I was in Chile which was faced with the problem of an inflation of 20 per cent a *month*. Now that is a different story altogether. To talk about that country trying to reduce its inflation rate at the rate of 1 per cent a year is silly. A country in that position has very few long-term contracts. One of the major effects of such a rapid rate of inflation is that people do not engage in long-term contracts which are contingent upon what the rate of inflation is going to be. Liquid resources are very small. Total money supply in Chile at that time amounted to three days' payment. It's a hand-to-mouth situation of the most extreme kind, because of course if prices are going up at 20 per cent a month you are going to make arrangements to keep to a very minimum the amount of cash or non-interest-earning assets you hold. And under those circumstances it seemed to me, as I argued then, as I would now, that the only sensible thing to do is a shock treatment, in which you make a very sharp move. You cut the figure right away and try to bring the inflation rate down to your long-term objective in a very short period.

These are not only hypothetical questions. We have a good deal of historical experience. There are two very important episodes in recent decades which illustrate how effective a shock treatment of that kind can be. One is the German Erhard episode in 1948, when Erhard terminated all wage and price controls over one weekend. He did it on a Sunday because the American, British and French occupation offices were closed and they would not be able to countermand his orders! A very similar situation occurred in Japan about the same time, in response to a mission from the United States headed by a banker from Detroit by the name of Dodge. The Japanese again used essentially shock treatment of a monetary reform, substituting a new money under new circumstances, cutting government spending sharply, getting the government's budget into a more tolerable position. In both cases you had very favourable results. Of course there were unfavourable aspects of the immediate shock, but they lasted only a short period, because you did not have long-term contracts built into the system that are the major source of difficulty in unwinding a high inflation.

Chile and Britain

In Chile they engaged in a shock treatment but only went halfway. They cut the growth of the money supply from something over

20 per cent a *month* to something over 10 per cent a month and brought the inflation rate down from 20 per cent a month to 10 per cent a month. I was very interested in the Chilean case because certain of the fundamental parameters were almost identical with those of the British case. The government deficit in Chile, which was being financed by printing money, was about 10 per cent of the national income. At that time the British government deficit, or borrowing requirement, was also roughly 10 per cent of the national income.

The reason why you are able to get away with so much lower an inflation rate of 20 per cent a *year* instead of 20 per cent a *month* is, first, that you are in a position to borrow half of that from overseas. Chile was not. Secondly, you did not have the long background of inflation as a result of which the Chileans had reduced their money holding to such small totals as three days' spending. In the United Kingdom you had a much larger total of liquid assets, so that inflation was a very much more productive tax in the United Kingdom than in Chile. To finance a budget deficit equal to 5 per cent of the national income by printing money thus required an inflation tax of only 20 or 25 per cent a year, and not 20 per cent a month as in Chile. But if Britain were to continue along these lines, those advantages would disappear, and you would be unable to borrow abroad. The tax would become progressively a less productive source of revenue, and to finance similar deficits you would have to engage in ever higher levels of inflation.

Modified shock treatment for Britain

The British case is not the American case and it is not the Chilean, German or Japanese cases – it is in between. And yet I think it is far enough along the way towards the German, Japanese or Chilean cases to make Britain a good candidate for a shock treatment, and not for a very gradualistic approach to cutting inflation at a slow rate over a long period. By shock treatment again I do not mean it would be feasible for you to bring the rate of inflation down to zero next month. But I see no reason why you should not try to establish guidelines and policies which would bring you into a roughly zero inflation within something like three to five years.

The instruments

What is required in order to do that? What do I mean by a shock treatment? The shock treatment can work in the British case if, and only if, it enables Britain to cut down the amount of money it has to create to finance its obligations. How can it do that?

Number one, and most importantly, you must cut government spending. I have no doubt that the absolute *sine qua non* of a non-inflationary policy in Britain is a cut. I do *not* mean a cut in the prospective *increase;* I mean a real cut in government spending and a cut that is substantial. That is the first requisite. Look at your figures now. You are spending something like 60 per cent of the national income through the government. Your explicit taxes are raising at most something like 50 per cent of the national income, and then only with systems of taxes which have severe disincentive effects on working, saving, and investing. The first step has to be to eliminate the need to finance that 10 per cent. That means a very minimum objective is to cut government spending from 60 down to 50 per cent of national income – something like that – within three years.

You could go further than that. The cut in government spending by a sixth is not a major magnitude. It would not reduce efficiency. There is little doubt that if you were to go through every government bureau in the United Kingdom and fire every sixth man, the productivity of the other five would go up rather than down. Your own experience of a three-day week in industry in February 1974 was very impressive evidence from that point of view. But the *political* difficulty is of course very severe, because the immediate initial effect of such cutting looks as if it is adding to unemployment. It is really not adding to unemployment. Rather it is rendering people available for *productive* employment instead of *unproductive* employment. Most of those people would be absorbed in a fairly brief period.

In any event, the only question that arises is: How can you cut government spending by that much? I have come to a very simple conclusion. There is only one way to do it. It is *not* by looking for places where money is wasted, *not* by seeking the worst workplaces, but *across the board*. You have to do it by saying: every department, every office is going to have a statutory obligation to make cuts year by year. It seems to me the only way to cut that is feasible is to say that this year every office, every department, is to be cut by 10 per cent; next year it is to be cut by another 10 per cent; and the year after that by another 10 per cent. And only then do you arrange the cuts as you will within departments. Only then can you consider the special case and have each department fight with every other department for a change in that total allocation. But once you start along the lines 'We're going to find waste', you will find that it is universal and then you open the door to the special interest behind each particular activity to bring their full pressure to bear; and you are then back in the whole story of special interest politics.

The public at large, I think, is much more likely to support a policy – indeed it has begun to support a policy – that says 'We are going to cut government spending from 60 per cent of the national income to 50 per cent in the next two or three years, and we are going to do it across the board'. If you start arguing with the public at large, by saying, 'We can get rid of a little bit of this department' or 'There's a wasteful activity here', it will be hopeless to get backing for it. That seems to me, from an economic point of view, to be the sensible way to go about your cuts in government spending.

Tax system reform by shock treatment

The second requisite of course is to reorganise the tax structure. Here again I think you really need a shock treatment and not a gradual move in one direction or another. There is nobody in your country or mine who does not recognise that our present tax system is a mess. It does not in practice achieve any of the objectives claimed for it. It taxes people who are in the same position differently, depending on the source of their income and on the accident of whether they can escape the tax.

One of the striking things that always seems a paradox to people from overseas who come to visit Britain is that they are puzzled as to why there are so many Rolls-Royces in a country on the verge of destruction, in which productivity has been going downhill, in which you have had great inefficiency, and in which the government has been dedicated these many years to egalitarianism. How come all these Rolls-Royces? And then you see the prices charged for second-hand Rolls-Royces. How can these people afford to pay £10,000, £20,000 for Rolls-Royces? The answer is very simple, as you know better than anybody else. It is the *cheapest* way in the world for anybody who has wealth to try to conserve it and also to buy transportation. If the alternative to investing that wealth in a Rolls-Royce is to invest it in income-yielding securities, most of the income is going to go to the tax collector, whereas it does not cost anything to have a Rolls-Royce. A man invests, say, £30,000 in a Rolls-Royce. If he invested it in income-earning securities, earning, say, 15 per cent, he would get a gross yield of £4,500 a year. If he's in the 98 per cent tax bracket he has only £90 a year left after tax to spend. So it costs him only £90 a year to have his Rolls-Royce all year! It's the cheapest form of transportation he can possibly buy! In addition, he has the advantage of an asset that will conserve some of its capital value. If he put it in government bonds, then every year it is going to be worth less, even aside from the amount that the government takes from him in taxes. And so your tax system discourages saving and investment. *It encourages wasteful, 'conspicuous' consumption.*

Again, if I ask what it costs an employer to employ a man, on the one hand, and what is the net yield to a man from being employed, on the other, I find both in your country and mine the tax system has introduced a very large wedge. I do not understand why people are puzzled by the phenomenon of simultaneous higher unemployment benefit and lower employment. Economic principles work: if you increase the demand for anything, the supply will grow to meet it. In your country and mine we have made it ever more attractive to be unemployed. *We have increased the demand for unemployment*, and the supply of unemployed has risen to meet that demand. On the other hand, we have imposed a heavy tax on employing anyone. So the result is that we have made employers unwilling to employ people. The wedge between the cost to the employer and the net return to the employee has become bigger and bigger.

Indexation and lower tax rates

I know what I would say in the United States, but I do not know enough of the British tax system to assess how I would go about reconstructing it in Britain. But I do know what the essential features are: first, indexation of the tax system so as to eliminate the tendency for inflation to push people up into ever-higher brackets and to eliminate the temptation for governments to use inflation as a way of financing their business. Secondly, a reduction in the special allowances and a sharp reduction along with that in the marginal rate of tax. You can raise the present revenue at vastly *lower* taxes if you apply the tax rates to the *whole* of the income, however earned and received, with no tax-free allowances. In the United States we have tax rates that go from 14 per cent at the bottom to 70 per cent at the top. You have rates which go up much higher than that. But if you eliminated the special deductions, exemptions and so-called loopholes from the income tax in the United States, you could raise the same revenue with the same personal exemptions with, I think, a flat rate of around 16 per cent. And in practice you would raise a lot more than that.

In a column I wrote a year or so ago[1] I demonstrated pretty conclusively, I think, that the United States government would get more revenue than it now gets from the personal income tax if it made no change in the law except to replace all tax rates above 25 per cent by 25 per cent. That change would yield *more* revenue because it would make it unprofitable for people to resort to the tax gimmicks and loopholes[2] they now use. *They would report more revenue.* The taxpayer would be better off and the Exchequer would be better off. One of the great mistakes people make in taxation policy is to treat the tax receipts of the government as if they corresponded to the cost of the taxes to the taxpayer. They do not. Because of the existence of the tax system, taxpayers are led to do all sorts of things (in the form of tax avoidance or evasion, including not working or engaging in occupations different from those they would engage in if taxes were lower) that are very costly to them but which yield no revenue to the government. It is this difference between the total cost to the taxpayer and the total receipts to the government that offers the opportunity for reductions that will benefit both the revenue and the taxpayer. This is the second shock treatment you badly need in the sense of a very substantial modification and change in the tax system.

I have only one other thing to say on how you get back to a non-inflationary state. I think it is right to put emphasis on how you hold down the quantity of money, but I think it is wrong to

[1] *Newsweek,* 12 April, 1976.

[2] [The effects of high tax rates in 'gimmicks and loopholes', etc., are discussed by Dr Barry Bracewell-Milnes in a Hobart Paper to be published in 1977. – ED.]

suppose that it is some kind of simple cure that can be introduced without affecting anything else. The real problem is to adjust the budget and government expenditures in such a way that it is feasible to hold down the rate of growth of the quantity of money.

II
Unwinding Government

Now let us suppose by some miracle you really had a political régime that was committed to moving away from the kind of welfare state, nationalised apparatus that Britain has, and that the US has been increasingly moving towards, and wanted to get to a largely free enterprise state in which people had a good deal more leeway about how they handled their own resources than they have now. What general principles can you think of that are relevant in proceeding from here to there?

Denationalisation by auctioning or giving away

Once again in some cases it is appropriate to get rid of it all at once. Most of these cases have to do with nationalisation of economic activities. I do not see any sense in saying 'We are going to "privatise" the steel industry piece meal' or 'We are going to sell off to the public 1 per cent of the steel industry each year'. The obvious thing to do with the steel industry, the railroads, and all those industries currently governmentally operated is to get rid of them by auctioning them off. Here there are various devices. At the moment it would be very hard to auction off the steel industry, because a Tory government did it once and then a Labour government renationalised it and anybody who buys it again would now be very uncertain that he would be able to retain ownership. One suggestion a number of people have made which I think makes a great deal of sense would be, not to auction it off, but to give it away, by giving every citizen in the country a share in it.

After all, the supposed argument is that the people of Great Britain own the steel industry; it is the property of all the citizens. Well, then, why not give each citizen his piece? Now you may say this raises some questions of feasibility. You might say 55 million shares are a lot of shares – in order to have a market in them you would have to re-introduce the farthing to enable people to buy and sell them. That's true.

A mutual fund

But it seems to me you could go at it in a very different way. You have not only the steel industry, but electricity, the BBC, railroads, road transport, etc. Suppose you constructed a mutual fund to which you assigned the shares in all these enterprises and then gave every one of the 55 million citizens of the United Kingdom a share in it. Now you are talking about magnitudes that are perfectly feasible.

I do not think individuals would regard a share in such a fund as derisory. And I do not see why that really is not the kind of approach you want to adopt because it meets every socialist value. These enterprises belong to the people; so we are going to give them to the people. This method has a big advantage. If you tried to auction these industries off individually, the *government* would get the revenue and it would waste it. But if you give it to the *people,* and you allow a market to be established, you would see in a very short period that this would unsnarl itself. In the first place, individuals would start to buy and sell the mutual shares they were given. In the second place, the mutual enterprise would see a market starting to be established in its stock. Perhaps you would need three or four mutuals. I am not going into details; I am trying to get at the principles. The fundamental principle is to do it in a way which gives the public at large a strong incentive to have it done, and not in a way which is simply another channel for the government to acquire revenue, as for example the UK government did in selling off the steel industry in the first place and then renationalising it. I think that kind of unwinding ought to be done all at once.

Towards profitability

But what if most of these industries now make a loss? They would not, once they were liberated from government control. You accomplish two purposes at once: you reduce the governmental deficit at the same time as you provide for a more efficient private economy. It may be reasonable, in 'privatising' them – in giving them to the mutual fund – for Parliament to provide a guarantee of a year or two of subsidy to enable them to get on their feet.

Let us leave aside the political issue and examine the economic issue. Suppose I say I want to auction off the steel industry. It may be that its market price as now nationalised is negative.

Therefore the auction procedure might be for the government to say: 'Who will take the steel industry off our hands for the least subsidy?' And similarly with the mutual fund. But from a political point of view it seems to me far more preferable to distribute it amongst the public at large than to try to do it by paying somebody to take it off your hands. And if the trade unions object, then give the nationalised industries to the unions.

III

Reduction of Government by Gradualism

Now I want to go on to the other class of policies where you need to proceed more gradually. These are the classic cases in which you have a government that has put individuals in a position where they are dependent on government bounty and in which you cannot really throw them out overnight. As a result of the welfare state measures that your country and my country have undertaken, millions of people today are dependent on the bounty of the state for their livelihood, and you cannot simply say we are going to cut that off overnight and throw them out on the street. The question here is, then, different. How do you set up arrangements which will simultaneously enable you to wind down those programmes but at the same time do not create great difficulties for settled expectations?

Vouchers or cash

Here I think the one principle which can be applied is that in general you can do so by trying to substitute vouchers or cash payments for services in kind or vouchers for particular groups in place of across-the-board payments and subsidies to everybody.

The voucher scheme has received perhaps most attention in education. Certainly it is, in my opinion, about the only feasible way to go from the government-dominated educational system we now have to the kind under which you have a free, competitive private-market educational system. That would be desirable. The virtues of the voucher system are in my opinion two-fold. One is that it introduces choice and enables competition to come into effect. That is the virtue that has been most discussed. But for the moment I want to discuss another virtue of a very different kind.

This is the possibility of winding things down, of reducing the fraction of the total costs borne by the government and thereby returning activities to the private sector. Ask anybody the abstract question: Is the case for governmental provision of education stronger in a poor society or in an affluent society? Or, is it more appropriate to expect parents to pay for the schooling of their children in a poor country or in a rich country? Almost everybody will answer: 'Obviously in a rich country it is more appropriate for parents to pay and there is more of a case for governmental provision in a poor country'. And yet *historically the relationship has been the other way round.*

In your country and my country, as we have become richer, the fraction of total educational expenditure that is borne by the state has gone *up*. Why? I believe the major reason is that governments have financed education through running educational *institutions*. They have set up schools and run them and therefore there has been no way in which private individuals could spend private money in a marginal way. As societies became more affluent people at large wanted to spend more on education but, given that government was providing the education, that led to more *government* provision.

Now one of the great virtues of a voucher system is that it makes it possible to move in the other direction. If you have a voucher of a fixed dollar or pound value, as the society gets richer people are encouraged to add to it, to use private provision in a marginal way to improve the kind of education and schooling their children get. You can think of the fraction of total governmental education expenditure declining over time so long as you can hold back the political pressures to raise the value of the vouchers. The political pressure then would not have only one place to go; it could at least be diverted by the opportunity to supplement state provision. Perhaps it would not in fact be diverted, but if you have a people committed to getting back to a free society it seems to me that is one of the great virtues of using vouchers.

Reverse income tax

The same thing goes for housing vouchers or medical vouchers. And of course it goes in a far more fundamental sense for eliminating the specific kinds of vouchers and getting a general voucher in the form of a reverse income tax. Now again, one of the virtues of a reverse income tax – (I once labelled it as a 'negative income tax' but the British use 'reverse income tax'. I must say I think negative income tax is more accurate because a negative tax is a subsidy but a reverse tax is – I don't know what a reverse tax is. Anyway, call it what you will.)[1] – its great virtue is that you do not have a system under which you provide medical care by special provision *in kind*, or provide housing and schooling by special services, and so on. In the first place you need a bureaucracy to administer each of these services and this establishes a very, very strong pressure for their maintenance and extension. I think it is true that the greatest forces in your country and in mine which have been promoting an extension of governmental welfare measures have not been the demand from the public at large, or the pressure of well-meaning reformers, but the internal pressure to extend the civil service to administer it.

I do not know how many people in Britain have read Pat Moynihan's book on the family assistance plan in the United States,[2] on the problems that arose when Mr Nixon at one stage proposed what was essentially a negative income tax. The theme of Moynihan's book is that that proposal was largely defeated by the welfare bureaucracy. They were the ones who really stirred up the trouble and defeated the proposal.[3] Look at it the other way: if you can put through a negative income tax as a *substitute* for, not an *addition* to, all the special piecemeal programmes, it has the great virtue that it will enable you to reduce the bureaucracy and reduce this pressure. And it also offers some hope that over

[1] [The term 'reverse income tax' was coined in IEA writings: *Policy for Poverty*, Research Monograph 20, 1970; *Choice in Welfare, 1970*, 1971; and others. The reason was simply that, if a tax was a payment to the fisc, a tax in reverse was a payment from the fisc. – ED.]

[2] Daniel P. Moynihan, *The Politics of a Guaranteed Income*, Random House, New York, 1973.

[3] [The proposal for an education voucher in the UK, and the moves to an experiment by Kent County Council, are being opposed mainly by the educational bureaucracy in the National Union of Teachers and elsewhere, or rather by the spokesmen for teachers. The voucher idea also met resistance in the Layfield Committee (*Local Government Finance: Report of the Committee of Enquiry*, Cmnd. 6453, HMSO, 1976): Ralph Harris and Arthur Seldon, *Pricing or Taxing?: Evidence to the Layfield Committee and a Critique of its Report*, Hobart Paper 71, IEA, 1976. – ED.]

a period you can gradually reduce the extent to which the government provides, e.g. schooling, as opposed to private provision.

The transition: special cases

One final point on the problem of the transition: in the United States we have tried to work in some detail on some of the special cases – social security, schooling, housing and so on. I cannot really do that for Britain but I think there are two fundamental principles: first, use the market mechanisms as much as you can in turning back the special provisions in kind; second, introduce gradualism of a type which can be made self-destructive.

Let me stop there and deal with anything you want to talk about.

IV
QUESTIONS AND ANSWERS

Cutting transfer payments

QUESTION: On the last point Professor Friedman made about welfare payments: much of the government's 60 per cent of the GNP is transfer payments, i.e. cash subsidies from the social rich to the social poor. And if we make a 10 per cent cut in government spending, where are you going to cut the subsidies the recipients get? You can't get it from the bureaucracy, anyway in the short term; you may in the long term. Would you say you should preserve their value in the short term while trying to introduce the voucher or the reverse tax? – we call it the tax credit now – in which case, of course, the bulk of the cuts is going to fall all the more heavily on other programmes like roads.

FRIEDMAN: No, I would not preserve the real value of transfer payments. If you can think of substituting a negative income tax it would cost far less than it costs you now if you replace your unemployment and health insurance arrangements, and so on, and bundle all of them together. The point is that all of the money you are now spending on transfer payments is not going to the poor. On the contrary, a lot of it is going to people who are not poor, and one of the main reasons is the proliferation of separate benefits. There is somebody who qualifies independently for benefits A, B, C, D, and E, and by the time you add them all together he is getting much more than anybody would think it appropriate to provide. So I think it is admirably appropriate to cut down spending on transfer payments.

Incidentally, I was not suggesting a cut of 10 per cent of government spending, but a cut of 10 per cent of the national income, which is a cut of 17 per cent on government spending, not 10 per cent. The aim is to bring government spending down from 60 per cent of the national income to 50 per cent. But I see no reason why that should not come in part out of the so-called transfer payments.

The cost of vouchers

MARJORIE SELDON: I'm often asked how you reconcile the need to cut government spending with the voucher system because if you give the voucher to every child the cost would be notionally about £140 million for the 5, 6 or 7 per cent of children educated privately. So you are, they say, adding to public expenditure.

FRIEDMAN: I have always answered that objection by saying I am going to calculate the size of the voucher by taking total current spending on schooling and dividing it by the *total* number of schoolchildren. I know from comparisons that the cost of private schooling, given comparable qualities, is roughly *half* the cost of the state system. Indeed, I may say this is a very interesting phenomenon. There is a sort of empirical generalisation that *it costs the state twice as much to do anything as it costs private enterprise*, whatever it is. My son[1] once called my attention to this generalisation, and it is amazing how accurate it is. Some studies have been done in the United States on the productivity in handling accounts of people in the governmental social security system and in the private insurance system and private commercial insurance agencies and, lo and behold, the ratio of productivity was 2:1. There are some cities and States in the United States which provide private profit-making fire departments; in Scottsdale, Arizona, for example, there is a private free enterprise fire department that protects citizens against fire by charging for it. And it turns out that it costs them half as much as it costs the municipal fire-fighting department. I don't want to overstate the exact 2:1 ratio, but roughly that is what it is. In schools

[1] David Friedman, Assistant Professor of Economics, Virginia Polytechnic Institute, Blacksburg, Virginia.

there is no doubt that there is at least a 2:1 difference. So if you took the total amount of money now being spent, divided it by the total number of children to get it, you do not add anything to expenditure. You would cut the voucher sums available to pupils in government schools by this 5 or 10 per cent, or whatever it is. But with that lower amount they could buy far *better* schooling than they are getting now, so everybody would be better off.

Experiment with vouchers

MRS. SELDON: Would you advocate experiment? You might not get the response of the market because people would say it's temporary and might come to an end. So you would not get the kind of responses you would have if you introduced it nationally. Would you therefore introduce it generally rather than in limited areas?

FRIEDMAN: I do not believe that is a question to be answered in the abstract. I think it is not going to be politically feasible to get it adopted overall unless it has been tried out in an experiment. I grant you an experiment will not be as satisfactory as a real commitment to it. But I would certainly be in favour of experiment because, again, if you were talking about a system that was going to be only 5 per cent better than another system, the difficulties of the experiment you point out would be very serious. But you are talking about a system that is going to be twice as efficient as the state system. So you can afford to have an *imperfect* experiment and still have very striking and effective results. Moreover, if you have an experiment for a five- or six-year period, it turns out that schooling does not require very long-term capital investment. You have had people setting up schools on a very temporary basis. So I think you would be surprised at the extent of the reaction you would get to an experiment. Unfortunately we have not been able to have a very good experiment in the United States so we do not have very much evidence for you.

Political intervention with a voucher system

STEPHEN EYRES: I was beginning to have second thoughts on vouchers and negative income tax as a way of introducing or restoring markets into hitherto state-provided areas because, although a market-oriented government may introduce a voucher system, this would not stop interventionist politicians imposing interventionist solutions to voucher schemes, such as advocating compensatory vouchers for specific interest groups or geographical areas. If we propose to phase out the vouchers over a period of time, the trouble is that people do not like having benefits taken away from them, and politicians could propose that the state part of the finance should be increased and not decreased.

FRIEDMAN: There are those problems, of course. The question is: What is the alternative? In higher education, I am 100 per cent with you. I think the right thing to do is to have loans: no doubt about that. But we are now talking about universal elementary and secondary education. I do not think fees-with-lower-taxes meets the political problems you are raising. On the contrary, I think it exacerbates them, because it very much encourages the introduction of fees in accordance with income. It encourages the use of fees as a supplementary method of taxing income, which is the counterpart of your compensatory voucher arrangement.

You are not solving the political problem by a fees-with-lower-taxes arrangement. If anything, you are making it more severe; and, so long as the state runs the schools, so long as taxes are used to subsidise the schools *per se*, you have no in-built mechanism to create a counter-move. You see, one of the virtues of the voucher system is that, insofar as it encourages private schools, it tends to build up a special group that has an interest in continuing the voucher system as opposed to going to state-supported schools. But you lose that advantage if you go the way of fees-with-lower-taxes.

Countering the 'vote motive'

CHRISTOPHER TAME: What is to prevent the politicians vying with each other to increase the monetary value of the vouchers?

FRIEDMAN: There's nothing to prevent that. And that raises a supplementary question of a different kind which I should have mentioned earlier. How do you prevent, or how do you act in such a way as to avoid, the 'vote motive'?[1] There is only one way I have seen that avoids it at all, and that is by somehow having a very strong public commitment to *aggregate* as opposed to

[1] [*The Vote Motive* is the title of a Hobart Paperback (No. 9) by Professor Gordon Tullock and Dr Morris Perlman, IEA, 1976. – ED.]

individual items. You see, the big way in which the vote motive operates, the defect of the political system, is that there is a tendency for each individual group to try to get its own way at the expense of the community at large. And so the special interest groups have a common interest in attacking the public at large.

There is one device we have been trying to work out in the United States that has been receiving wide attention. We of course have a written constitution, which you do not. We have tried to institute constitutional provisions setting a limit to the maximum amount of money as a fraction of the national income that governments may spend in all directions. Governor Reagan in California a couple of years ago sponsored Proposition 1, which was to be an amendment to the State of California constitution. It was to limit State spending to the same percentage of the State income as it was then, with gradual reduction in that percentage over time. It failed at adoption by a rather narrow margin, something like 47 to 53 per cent. A similar provision is going to be on the ballot in Michigan this Fall as an amendment to the Michigan constitution. In three or four other States a movement along this line is under way. In addition, a number of Congressmen have introduced proposals for a Federal constitutional amendment along these lines, and a committee of the Southern Governers Conference has been assigned to work on this problem and has prepared a constitutional amendment to the Federal constitution along this line and it is going to try to get the backing of Southern Governors for it.

The problem is that the only way you can beat the vote motive is by generally accepted limitations on the scope of government. They can be written constitutional limitations or unwritten limitations, as they are in the UK. That is what limited the scope of government in the 19th century in both our countries. I think it is very difficult to conceive of doing it now by limiting the *activities* governments can engage in, but it is still feasible to do it by limiting total government *spending*. What you need is to be able to do something which in the first place wraps together all the particular difficulties for individuals into one big whole, generalises them and enables you to achieve something by a one-time crusade and does not require eternal vigilance. That is the great virtue in the United States of being able to get a constitutional amendment. Once you get it through, it is difficult to overturn, and you do not have to keep working at it all the time. You in Britain do not have that possibility. If, for example, we in the United States could get a constitutional amendment limiting total federal government spending, let us say, to 25 per cent of the national income, *you force the special interest groups to fight one another*.

Evidence on effectiveness (speed) of changes

QUESTION: On your point about what is necessary to move resources from unproductive to productive units, have you any evidence at all on the rate at which that shift is feasibly possible?

FRIEDMAN: If you look at the kind of cases I was quoting, the most extreme where this was done in one fell swoop were the German and Japanese. The initial position had become very bad and this was the kind of case that Ralph Harris was citing earlier[1] about the short-term pessimists who think it has to get worse before it gets better. But it is remarkable how rapid the recovery was, on a very broad scale, both in Japan and in Germany. I am under the impression that Britain is in a position where you can have an equally rapid improvement, and that is because you are so bad now. In Britain before World War II real income per head was double that in Germany and France, but today real income per head in Germany and France is double that in Britain. You can make very rapid progress under any circumstances where there is a large gap between your position and that of other similar countries. The reason why Japan was able to have such a very rapid rate of growth over so long a period, and more recently that has been true of Brazil as well, is that the initial level from which she started was so much lower than that of other countries.

Psychological shock?

QUESTION: As in Germany, so in Japan, the crucial thing was not the mechanism but the psychological shock which altered people's

[1] [This is a reference to the diverse sectional resistances to the 1944 Education Bill. 'We decided at the very outset to make the [educational] reform as comprehensive as possible, and if there were any nettles to get a good bunch of them in our arms and not be stung by a little one. That policy has proved extremely successful . . . because the more nettles you collect the more they sting one another and the less they sting you.' – Quoted from Ralph Harris, *Politics without Prejudice*, Staples Press, London, 1956. – ED.]

attitudes to wealth and everything else. I do not see how you are going to get that psychological shock in Britain at the moment.

FRIEDMAN: Brazil perhaps will fit your case better, because there was no such psychological shock. There it was all mechanism. It was the introduction of indexation, which brought some freeing of prices plus a floating exchange rate.

A Note on Readings

(A) GALBRAITH'S MAIN WORKS

A Theory of Price Control, Harvard University Press, 1952.

American Capitalism: The Concept of Countervailing Power, Hamish Hamilton, 1952; Penguin, 1963.

Economics and the Art of Controversy, Vintage Books, New York, 1959.

The Great Crash, 1929, Hamish Hamilton, 1958; Penguin, 1962.

The Affluent Society, Hamish Hamilton, 1958; Penguin, 1962.

The New Industrial State, Hamish Hamilton, 1967; Penguin, 1969.

Economics and the Public Purpose, André Deutsch, 1974; Penguin, 1975.

Economics, Peace and Laughter, André Deutsch 1971; Penguin, 1975.

Money: Whence It Came, Where It Went, Houghton Mifflin, New York, 1975; Penguin, 1977.

(B) SOME OTHER WRITINGS ON GALBRAITH'S CENTRAL THEMES (*in addition to works cited in the text)*

Brozen, Yale (ed.), *Advertising and Society*, New York University Press, 1974.

Collection of empirical studies of the significance and reality of advertising, yielding a very different impression from that of Galbraith.

— *The Competitive Economy*, General Learning Press, Morristown, New Jersey, 1975.

Collection of empirical studies leading to contrary conclusions to Galbraith's on the structure of the American economy.

Hayek, F. A., 'The Non Sequiter of the "Dependence Effect" ', *Southern Economic Journal*, April 1961; reprinted in Hayek, *Studies in Philosophy, Politics and Economics*, Routledge & Kegan Paul, London, and University of Chicago Press, Chicago, 1967.

Brief treatment of Galbraith's central argument in *The Affluent Society*. Argues that wants labelled as not 'original' or 'autonomously' arrived at are not therefore on such grounds undesirable, unworthy or unimportant. Criticises Galbraith's failure to distinguish between the general cultural conditioning of wants and producers' influence on specific items of consumption.

Kirzner, Israel M., *Competition and Entrepreneurship*, University of Chicago Press, 1973.

'Austrian' view of the competitive process and the role of the entrepreneur; the distinction between managerial and entrepreneurial functions, the contribution of advertising, etc. Criticises Galbraith's idea of 'original', autonomous wants untouched by advertising. Argues that consumers' demand is inconceivable without information (advertising), 'product' and 'information' are inseparable, and persuasion is an inevitable part of information.

Rothbard, Murray N., 'Professor Galbraith and the Sin of Affluence', in *Man, Economy and State,* vol. 2, Nash Publishing, Los Angeles, 1970; orig. D. Van Nostrand, Princeton, New Jersey, 1962.

Professor Rothbard criticises *The Affluent Society* as 'replete with fallacies . . . dogmatic assertions and time-honoured rhetorical devices in place of reasoned argument' (p. 840). Focusses on its conceptions of 'poverty', 'affluence', 'excess' affluence, misunderstanding of the declining marginal utility of goods, the deterministic view of the power of advertising, and its moralistic assertions.

'The Sumptuary Manifesto', *Journal of Law and Economics,* October 1959 (Anonymous).

Satire on *The Affluent Society* in the form of a manifesto supporting a political programme aimed at 'liberating mankind from their insane preoccupation with material comforts of low marginal urgency'.

Tullock, Gordon, 'The New Theory of Corporations', in Erich Streissler et al (eds.), *Roads to Freedom: Essays in Honor of F. A. von Hayek,* Routledge and Kegan Paul, London, 1969.

Discussion of the evidence for and against the Berle and Means – and Galbraithian – notion of the autonomy of management. Concludes that the disciplines of the capital market and the competitive process instil profit maximisation as the predominant managerial motive to countervail the 'growth' and 'bureaucratic' impulses.

Synopsis

1. No scientific studies have validated Galbraith's analysis: it yields no predictions about the behaviour of enterprise, industry or of the economy that have been tested and found correct. The experience of industry in Britain and America is inconsistent with his assertions about the economy.

2. British and American economists who have examined his work have been severely critical of its over-simplifications and over-generalisations.

3. Unlike Adam Smith, Keynes and other leaders of economic thinking, Galbraith has not attracted the support of economists to form a school of economic thought. His is a one-man crusade.

4. *The Affluent Society* was not about methods to help the poor but about expanding the power of government.

5. The concept of 'countervailing power' is defective: big business and big labour can conspire to exploit the consumer. It is also unfounded: the largest concentration of union power may be in industries with little concentration of employer power.

6. Galbraith has replaced 'countervailing power' by the 'technostructure' as an explanation of the modern economy. It also is controverted by evidence, notably that of Demsetz on the returns from investment in defence-orientated industries, the relative stability of technostructure-orientated firms, and the supposed maximisation of sales rather than profits. The Galbraith view that industry enlists government in creating the 'technostructure' is the opposite of the truth that the government initiates and promotes it.

7. Galbraith must be seen not as a scientist seeking explanations but as a missionary seeking converts.

8. His work is directed at the mass of people who it is expected will look to intellectuals to guide government in replacing entrepreneurs.

9. His denigration of consumer choice in markets is a prelude to claims by paternalistic technocrats to know what the consumer wants. The Galbraith approach ignores the distinction between the economic market, in which people receive what they pay for, and the political market, in which the politician decides what to give them.

10. The move away from the world of Galbraith of state economy to a market-based economy in Britain requires, urgently, the mastery of inflation by gradual reduction of the rate of monetary growth over a period of years to the underlying growth in real output.

11. To make reduction of monetary growth feasible requires a reduction of government expenditure from 60 per cent to at most 50 per cent of national income as currently measured by across-the-board cuts in departmental budgets.

12. The longer-term goal of giving British citizens an incentive to save, invest and produce requires (1) reconstruction of the tax system by reducing marginal tax rates and by indexing, (2) denationalisation, not gradually but promptly by auctioning government-owned industries, or by giving them to the public at large through mutual funds, (3) replacement of welfare, other services in kind and generalised subsidies by vouchers or income-related cash. The voucher system would not only introduce choice and competition but also facilitate the required reduction in government.

13. A negative (reverse) income tax in place of current welfare measures would help to reduce government services in kind, with their bureaucratic pressure for expansion, by cash to people with lower incomes, requiring smaller government expenditure and bureaucracy.

14. Since the costs of state activities are much higher than in the market, experiments with systems of choice and competition would suffice to show their striking superiority.

15. Vouchers are superior to fees with lower taxes because they build special interest-groups opposed to state bureaucracy.

16. The only ultimate way to reduce the use of the vote motive for political advantage is to reduce the scope of government.